STORMS OF PERFECTION

In Their Own Words

STORMS OF PERFECTION

In Their Own Words

ANDY ANDREWS

Network Marketing Distributor

INTERNET SERVICES CORPORATION
Charlotte, NC

Distributed To The Trade By
NATIONAL BOOK NETWORK, INC.

Books are available at quantity discounts to schools, civic organizations, corporations, and small businesses. For information please write to: Marketing Division, Lightning Crown Publishers, P.O. Box 17321, Nashville, TN 37217.

Published in Nashville, Tennessee
by Lightning Crown Publishers
P.O. Box 17321, Nashville, TN 37217.

The Bible verses used in this publication are from the New American Standard Version and the New King James Version. Used by permission.

Printed in the United States of America.
FIRST EDITION

First Printing	11,500	June 1991
Second Printing	17,000	July 1991
Third Printing	17,000	September 1991

SECOND EDITION

| First Printing | 75,000 | March 1992 |

Library of Congress Catalog Card Number: 91-062009
ISBN 0-9629620-1-5

Editor: Robert D. Smith
Book Design by Payne Art Design Agency
Back Cover Photo by Mark Martin

LIGHTNING CROWN PUBLISHERS

P.O. BOX 17321 • NASHVILLE, TN 37217

TABLE OF CONTENTS

FOREWORD

When I first met Andy Andrews, I admired his ability to make people laugh. That certainly hasn't changed.

But when I read *Storms of Perfection*, I developed a newfound admiration for Andy's ability to get people to talk about their deepest feelings.

You see, nothing strikes harder at self-esteem and personal worth than those times when rejections or problems seem to overwhelm you. Yet, during those worst moments, you find out what you really are.

That's what the people in this must-read book allow you to see. Considering who many of them are, it is nothing short of remarkable that Andy has been able to get these men and women to reveal their hurts throughout these pages.

Reading this book also helped me to see another side of Andy Andrews. I have come to the realization that Andy is able to touch people - through his comedy and now through this book - because he has faced an extraordinary number of hurts and rejections himself.

To see him on stage, you would never know that this boy who was reared as a PK (preacher's kid - and that is enough to stymie some people), was still a teenager when both his parents died. Left to support a younger sister, Kristi, he made the commitment to continue his fledgling career in comedy.

Everybody, it seemed, told him, "get a REAL job." People said, "the chances are one in a million that you will ever make it." Others chimed, "you're never going to do anything in this business."

It wasn't easy. Andy remembers eating hamburgers at fast-food restaurants with his long-time manager, Robert Smith, because cheeseburgers were 10 cents more than the hamburgers.

One time he was so broke, Andy went to a pawn shop in Birmingham and hocked some of his clothes and silverware, just so he and Robert could go pay their $26 phone bill before it was cut off (it's a little difficult to book a comedy act without a telephone).

When they weren't staying in dingy motels on the road, they lived in a dingy basement in Birmingham. "We ate lots of soup," Andy remembers, "and lots of the time we didn't eat anything."

The struggles have continued. As a young comedian, for example, he was simply "too clean." He was told that his act wouldn't work on college campuses. Of course, since then he has received several "Comedian of the Year" and "Entertainer of the Year" awards from the National Association for Campus Activities.

He was told that he was not the right kind of entertainment for cruise ships, but now he is a featured performer on the world's largest ship, the S.S. Norway!

The experts said he was too "modern" to go over with country music crowds, yet he has toured with the likes of Kenny Rogers, Randy Travis and Barbara Mandrell.

At the same time, he was too country and too wholesome to tour with pop or rock artists, but has toured with people such as Joan Rivers and Cher.

A lot of people said he would never make it. I wonder what they think when they switch on their televisions to see him performing on national TV or headlining a command performance before President and Mrs. Bush. What do those dreamkillers think when Andy is featured in *Variety*, *USA Today*, *Country America* Magazine or on Paul Harvey's broadcasts?

Ironically, so many people look at Andy Andrews today and think "he's got it made." People don't know how hard it has been for him. In fact, it was after a painful rejection that Andy came up with the idea for this book. I am grateful that he had enough experience with turn-downs to understand that all those people with "charmed" lives had their share of tough times before there was any promise of success.

I am grateful, also, that his wife Polly helped him. Because she has endured so many hard times as Andy's career grew, she also has a special understanding of how difficult it is to face rejection.

Above all, I appreciate the roadmap Andy has provided. Through the pages of this book, I believe any reader can find the answers to overcome those times of monumental rejection and hurt. This is the message that people need - now more than ever.

Storms of Perfection symbolizes what J. Willard Marriott, the great hotel founder, once wrote:

> Good timber does not grow with ease; the stronger
> the wind, the stronger the trees.

Thanks, Andy, for this book and for helping people understand, once again, the true price of success.

– Dexter Yager
Charlotte, North Carolina

PREFACE

I was seven years old, barely keeping pace as my father strode purposefully through the woods, the dry brush crackling under our feet. August was rarely pleasant in the deep South, but this year had been especially hot; especially dry.

Walking the densely forested stand of timber that day, young as I was, I was acutely aware of my father's mood. The month-long drought our area was experiencing had him worried. I watched in silence as he broke dry twigs from seemingly lifeless trees and examined the wilting, dull color of the new growth under them. We hiked through the dust of the parched creek bed, following it to the beaver pond where our family often came for picnics. The pond was nearly empty and the beaver lodge, usually a site of frantic activity, stood abandoned on dry land.

Without warning, the wind shifted. And with the change in direction came a rapid increase in velocity and a perceptible drop in the temperature. It became cool within a matter of seconds, as the wind, whistling above, threatened to send branches crashing down around us. Lightning and thunder worked the atmosphere almost simultaneously, creating explosions of light and sound that terrified me. My father, his arms wrapped around me tightly, was also afraid...and grateful.

He was grateful for this violent performance of nature and the hope of water that came with it. As the trees bent with the wind and the thunder covered my cries, my father sat down, pulled me into his lap and said, "Don't worry. You'll be all right. Something good is going to come out of this. Be still. Be patient."

While he was comforting me, the rain came. Not with the gentle drops I had seen in the past, but in wild, silver sheets bursting all around us. It wound through the limbs and leaves, over rocks and deep into the tangled thickets leaving nothing untouched.

And then, as suddenly as it had begun - it was over. The thunder and lightning and wind and rain were gone, their energy exhausted. It was still again, but even at my young age, I noticed a difference. The forest wasn't just still...it was calm.

With his hand, my father wiped the drops of water from my face. Only my deep sobs betrayed the presence of tears, not raindrops, on my cheeks. Then he smiled, wrung out the front of his shirt, and motioned toward the pond. "It'll fill back up now," he said, "and those beavers will be able to spend the winter here like they'd planned."

We turned in time to see a doe and her fawn drinking from the already flowing creek. The frogs had started their own chorus as we headed for home. "Ahh," my father breathed deeply, "everything just smells clean, doesn't it?" And it did. The very air, which only a short time ago had been hot and dirty, now seemed almost sweet. "Let's sit down by this big oak, Son," he said quietly, "I have something to tell you."

I snuggled in beside him, and in very nearly a whisper, he began. "You know," he said, watching me from the corner of his eye, "you weren't the only one scared a little while ago. Those deer were afraid, too. The squirrels huddled together as close as they could get and what with all the crashes and booms, well, I'm pretty sure the rabbits were worried. But now, something important has happened. The very event that frightened everyone in the forest turned out to be exactly what they needed."

Do you hear the birds?" I nodded. "Remember how quiet they were before the rain? Now they're hopping around, chirping, drinking from puddles, and feasting on the worms that come out only when the ground is wet. The fish in the pond have more oxygen to breathe and cooler water to swim in. The dust that was on all the plants has been washed away so they are much cleaner for the rabbits and deer to eat. Nobody likes dirty food."

"In fact, Son, all of us are better off now than we were an hour ago. Just because of the storm. What looked like the worst - turned out to be the best. It was a storm of perfection."

*   *   *

My dad has been gone now for well over a decade, but I can remember that day in the woods as if it had happened this morning. Writing this now, I couldn't begin to count the instances I've had reason to recall his words. There have been many storms in my life; and some were more terrifying than that day when I was seven. I do try, however, to keep my father's lesson in my heart. And it is easy to hear him tell me, "Don't worry. You'll be all right. Something good is going to come out of this. Be still. Be patient. It's only a storm of perfection."

Dedicated to the memory of my father,
Larry Andrews,
who told me on more than one occasion, "Do it if you really
want to, but if you start--you will finish"!

Also to Charles Raymond Floyd, Robert Henderson,
Norse Luker, Haywood Perkins, Dick Rollins,
Billy Sartin, and Wade Ward.

Because of their example,
quitting was never an option.

SPECIAL THANKS

I am especially indebted to my wife, Polly, and my manager, Robert D. Smith, for their encouragement, patience, and administrative skills.

My sincere gratitude goes to Sandie Dorff for the long hours spent coordinating the correspondence for this book; Martha Luker for late night over the phone editing; and to Theresa Brown and Evelyn Shriver for their invaluable contacts.

Thanks also to Barney Andrews, Gloria Ashcroft, Evelyn Barty, Harry Brooks, Brent Burns, Barbara Buzzell, Jaque Caplan, Rick and Sue Carper, Dan Corte, Chaz Corzine, Danny the UPS man, Charles Duncan, Jean Ferrari, Tim and Connie Foley, Renae Gibson, Jay Goldberg, Glen Grabski, Ward Grant, Lib Hatcher, Jeff Harr, Kathy Harris, Brig and Lita Hart, Susan Hennessy, Sylvia Hundley, Lois Hunter, Kaye Isaacs, Kelly Junkerman, Leslie Lamb, Sybil Light, Francine Lipsman, Mark and Wanda Llewellyn, Debbie Marshall, Dorothy Melvin, Barbi Miller, Maggie Monaghan, Rodney Morgan, Pat Mullins, Nancy Niekro, Sherrie Nichols, W.T. Oliver, Susan Palmer, Kevin and Glenda Perkins, Rob Pincus, Bubba and Sandy Pratt, Rozene Pride, Riki Rafner, Ingrid V. Raymon, Judy Riley, Gene Roy, Ron Scalf, Teresa Shelly, Sally Sickles, Ray Shelide, Karl Soderland, C.K. Spurlock, Stacey Stakley, Cherry Starr, Linda Stewart, Jay Stradley, Sam Thompson, Judy Tillis, Angie Wallace, Roger White, Jeff Witjas, Don and Nancy Wilson, Orlando Wilson, Dexter and Birdie Yager, and Doyle Yager.

AUTHOR'S NOTE

I have always been interested in successful people. Not necessarily wealthy people, but people who, by force of will, complete a chosen task and often do so in a spectacular way. What makes them different from us, and are they, in fact, different at all?

After researching the lives of some of these people, a curious pattern began to develop. It wasn't that they were all well educated. Most, in fact, were not. Some didn't receive support from their families. Age, race, and gender didn't seem to matter. Neither did the presence or absence of money connect to any degree the men and women I studied. There was only one constant; one common thread which invariably wove through the lives of all these people.

Problems. They had all experienced incredible problems!

These problems occurred at various stages in their lives and manifested themselves in an endless number of ways. Rejection, illness, poverty, self-doubt, and imprisonment were but a few on the long list I compiled.

But surely, I thought, problems can't be the only factor involved in attaining greatness. Problems in and of themselves couldn't lead directly to success, could they? The answer is obviously no, of course not. These people all eventually found the winner's circle because they refused to quit looking! They didn't shy away from obstacles the way most of us do. They found a way around, tunneled through, or simply kept chipping away at the obstacle until it was no longer there!

Some of the stories I found were testaments to those who ignore the words, "No, it can't be done." A case in point is that of Dr. Laurence J. Peter, author of *The Peter Principle: Why Things Always Go Wrong*. In 1964, after submitting his book manuscript to thirty-one different publishers, it was finally accepted by William Morrow & Co. Congratulations are still in order for Dr. Peter. The book sold more than 200,000 copies in its first year and remained on the <u>New York Times</u> best-seller list through 1970. Today, more than twenty-five years later, the book has been translated into thirty-eight languages and is still selling briskly.

Other instances I uncovered weren't quite so thrilling. The lessons they taught, however, are just as real. Another writer named John Kennedy Toole wrote a novel about life in a southern city called *A Confederacy of Dunces*. It was so unanimously rejected by publishers that, in 1969, Mr. Toole committed suicide. His mother refused to give up on the book. She sent it out again and again. The book was returned to her every time...rejected. At last it was accepted by the Louisiana State University Press. In 1980, it won the Pulitzer Prize for fiction.

These examples should encourage us--and at the same time be a cause for alarm! What might we accomplish if we simply refuse to quit? And what are we missing every time we do?!

Some time ago, I began contacting people from all walks of life who were enormously successful in their chosen field. I specifically asked, "What was the worst rejection or biggest problem that you had to overcome before you became successful?" Even now, I am not sure what I was expecting, but as the letters came in, I became more and more convinced that these men and women had become great due to their attitudes toward the difficulties in their lives. Here then, in their own words, are their stories...

ANDY ANDREWS
Gulf Shores, Alabama

DR. NORMAN VINCENT PEALE

MINISTER/AUTHOR

...has written thirty-six books which have been translated into forty languages. Along with his wife, Ruth Stafford Peale, he is publisher of the inspirational monthly magazine, GUIDEPOSTS.

When I received Dr. Peale's letter last October, I immediately had a copy made and sent it to a friend. He was, at the time, suffering unwarranted criticism in his life. And that is how, before this book was ever published--a letter was already "working."

As my editors discussed the occupation to be used as a description of Dr. Peale on this page, no one could agree. "Minister/Author" seemed a terribly inadequate label for a man of his accomplishments. And as a matter of fact, it still does!

At the age of ninety-four, Norman Vincent Peale is still affecting millions of people in a positive way. His magazine, GUIDEPOSTS, is enjoyed every month by over 15 million readers (of which I am one). Over 31 million copies of his inspirational booklets are distributed yearly, and he maintains a full schedule of speaking engagements. He has received twenty-two honorary doctoral degrees and is one of the few private citizens in history to be honored in a White House ceremony where President Reagan presented him with the Presidential Medal of Freedom.

Interestingly enough, Dr. Peale might have achieved much less in his life had he yielded to an opportunity presented him years ago...the opportunity to quit.

Norman Vincent Peale
1025 Fifth Avenue
New York, NY 10028

Mr. Andy Andrews
P. O. Box 2761
Gulf Shores, AL   36547

Dear Andy:

I suffered rejection when I wrote a book called
The Power of Positive Thinking. Actually, I wanted to
call it "The Power of Faith," but my publishers
insistently demanded that I change the title to a
phrase I had unconsciously written in the book, "The
power of positive thinking."

It soon, to my surprise, hit the best seller
lists; in fact, it was on the New York Times best
seller list for 186 weeks, which at that time was a
record. This projected me into the most vehement
criticism I ever received. I considered the book a
vitally Christian book, but some ministers castigated
me as an archconservative, a tool of capitalistic
interests, who was turning Christianity into a way to
get rich. One bishop, a scholarly and gifted man,
usually dispassionate and objective, became quite
intemperate in his attacks on the book and upon me
personally. Many ministers even preached against some
terrible thing labeled "Pealism." And one
distinguished pulpiteer called my work a perversion of
the Christian religion. This hue and cry became so
violent that I actually wrote out my resignation from
the ministry. Though my church stood by me valiantly.

I took a train upcountry to see my aged father who
perceived that something was bothering me. And he,
even in that remote area, knew of the scathing attack
upon me had penetrated.

So my father, sitting in his rocking chair said,
"Norman, you have always been true and loyal to Jesus
Christ. You believe in and preach Bible truths. You
have always been in the mainstream of Christianity,
never following any temporary faddism. You have united
the pastoral office with the best in the scientific and
healing arts. You have blazed new pathways of positive
thinking to counter the old destructive negatives. You
are my son, and your old father who has known good men
and not so good men for eighty years and more, both in

and out of church, says you are a good and loyal minister of Jesus Christ." He was silent and thoughtful for a long minute. "Besides, and remember this, the Peales never quit. It would break my heart if one of my sons was a quitter, afraid to stand up and face any situation."

My father was a gentle-spirited man, and in all my life I had never heard him use any expression that included a swearword. Imagine my shock when he said, "And Norman, there's just one thing more."

"What is it, Dad?" I asked.

"Tell'em to go to hell," he declared, to my astonishment.

Stepping into another room, I tore up my resignation and threw it into the wastebasket. Needless to say, I came away fortified in spirit.

The books has sold upwards of 20 million copies worldwide and has become in book statisticians' opinion, one of the few books in American history that has sold the most. The title has become part of the language and actually part of the culture not only in America but the world.

A lady who was at one time president of the National Council of Churches, Cynthia Weddell, meeting a friend of mine said, "How's Norman?" And the friend replied, "He is fine." And added, "He has outlived his critics." "No," said Mrs. Weddell, "he has outloved them."

In every rejection you learn something and I learned that if you just go about your business and love people and not hate anyone that you ultimately gain a victory. Now it so happens that very few people criticize me wherefrom I deduce that perhaps I am slipping.

Cordially yours,

Norman Vincent Peale

NVP:sel

KENNY ROGERS

ENTERTAINER

...is the top grossing concert attraction in the world according to AMUSEMENT BUSINESS magazine. He has won virtually every major award in the music industry and has recorded thirty-six gold and multi-platinum albums.

Kenny Rogers holds a major distinction in my life. His concert is, to this day, the only one for which I have ever bought a ticket. I was in college at the time and Kenny had just begun to sell out arenas. As I sat there that night in my "rafter" seat, cheering Kenny with ten thousand other fans, it never crossed my mind that one day I would be privileged to work with him.

And working with Kenny is a pleasure. There is an old show business axiom which states that "the attitude of the crew reflects the attitude of the star." It's absolutely true. The people with whom Kenny has surrounded himself are, quite simply, among the best in the industry. They deal with every act on his tour in exactly the same manner: Whatever is needed, whatever must be done--no problem is too big to handle!

The Kenny Rogers that exists off-stage is personable, friendly, and never satisfied with his golf game! He had his own 18 hole golf course built around his house in Georgia. And he doesn't just play at home. His clubs are a permanent part of his traveling baggage. I have never, *ever* seen anyone who is "into" golf like Kenny.

The time Kenny spent writing his letter for this book will be appreciated by many people. And as one of the few entertainers to ever receive the "Horatio Alger Award," he is acutely aware of the secret to his success. The secret for Kenny Rogers, who grew up in a Houston housing project and is now one of the biggest stars in the world, has been his steadfast desire to persevere.

ROGERS
PRODUCTIONS

Dear Andy,

What a great concept! I'm sure that anyone who has had even a modicum of success has had an equal number of failure stories to tell.

I remember how I felt in 1976, when the First Edition broke up. We'd had a good run, nearly ten years, with quite a few hits, concerts and television appearances, even our own TV show...all the trappings of success in the music business. I figured it would last forever. In fact, I was counting on it, so when it didn't last, I was devastated. I was also broke, in debt to the tune of $65,000. And while I planned on a solo career, my prospects were uncertain at best.

The situation wasn't what you'd call ideal, but it could have been a lot worse. For one thing, I had met Marianne when the First Edition appeared on "Hee-Haw"; she had been a regular on that show since 1974. When we married the year after the group broke up, my career was at its lowest ebb. But when I realized that Marianne loved me anyway, I learned an incredibly valuable lesson. I learned that success wasn't the most important thing to me; I learned that having someone who loved me for the right reasons, who loved me for who I was rather than what I was, was far more significant. Knowing that we could be happy with absolutely nothing was actually a tremendous relief.

Ken Kragen, a long time friend and manager, still believed in me as an artist. In 1977, after I had released a couple of solo records, we put out "Lucille," which was a huge success and truly the catalyst in the resurgence of my career. I have always maintained that a person needs only three things to have a stable life--someone to love, something to do, and something to look forward to. I had all of those things. But the truth is, I don't think success would have happened had there not been failure as well.

Andy, good luck with this project.

Your friend,

Kenny Rogers

BROOKS ROBINSON

FORMER MAJOR LEAGUE THIRD BASEMAN

...has been called the greatest third baseman in the history of baseball. He was elected to the Hall of Fame in 1983 and is now involved in marketing with Crown Central Petroleum.

Brooks Robinson was my father's favorite baseball player. It didn't make any difference that the Orioles weren't his team-- Brooks Robinson was his player. I can remember the incredible catch Mr. Robinson made to end a World Series game. It was a fast move to his right and as if by magic, the ball was in his glove. Just that quickly, the game was over. I remember the catch because of my dad's reaction. He talked about it for weeks. He gave us slow-motion demonstrations. You'd have thought he caught the ball himself.

Playing third base in Little League was almost a curse for me. "Brooks leans toward the plate when the pitcher winds up. Brooks holds the bat higher. Dive for the ball like Brooks does." I heard these kind of things every day!

And it wasn't only my dad. Other fathers were saying the same things to their boys. Every generation has its baseball hero, and for my father and his friends, Brooks Robinson was the one. He was the example they held up to their sons as to how they should play on the field--and how they should conduct themselves off it. "Brooks is the best," they'd say. And even now, after almost twenty years, he may still be.

Crown Central Petroleum Corporation
Refiners / marketers of petroleum products & petrochemicals

One North Charles Street • P.O. Box 1168 • Baltimore, Maryland 21203 • (301) 539-7400

Mr. Andy Andrews
Post Office Box 2761
Gulf Shores, Alabama 36547

Dear Andy,

In June of 1955, the day I graduated from high school, I signed a professional baseball contract with the Baltimore Orioles. After two seasons, in the minor leagues, I made the team and in 1957, I was at third base on opening day. Two weeks later, I had a knee operation and missed two months of the season. After recovering, I headed back to the minors.

In 1958, I spent the entire season in Baltimore, but hitting .238 didn't really distinguish me as a major league player. Putting things in a positive light, however, I was able to look on that as my first full year in the majors and certainly something I could build on for 1959. I can remember saying to myself, "Okay. You've got a full season under your belt; '59 is going to be your year!"

Heading to Florida for spring training that next year, all I could think about was "This is the year for Brooks Robinson to step to the fore front!"

Things went well in Florida and when opening day rolled around, I was indeed on third base. The first month of the season passed uneventfully until, on May 18th, I received the shock of my young baseball life. Paul Richards, our manager, called me early that morning and asked me to have breakfast with him. Since it was my twenty-second birthday, I was excited. I just thought he was treating me to celebrate the occasion!

In the coffee shop we sat down at a table and ordered. Richards looked me in the eye. "Brooks," he said, taking a deep breath, "we're sending you back to the minors."

He proceeded to tell me that I was going to our AAA affiliate in Vancouver, B. C. Explaining that since I had missed most of spring training due to an Army obligation, he wanted me to play my way back into shape with no pressure involved.

I stared at him and listened, his words sounding as though they were coming from a tunnel. My dreams were shattered, my ego deflated, and I was just plain scared. Though he promised I'd be back with the Orioles soon, I knew that more often than not, a guy was sent to the minors just so they could forget about him. I'd seen it happen many times before. I was as low as I've ever been. Needless to say, this was not a Happy Birthday!

Well, Andy, a curious thing happened and it taught me a lesson I've never forgotten. What I perceived to be a disaster of the greatest magnitude, the worst news of my young life, turned out to be the best thing that could have happened to Brooks Robinson!

My time in Vancouver was a success. We had a terrific team and I played extremely well when I was there. In July, I returned to the major leagues to stay--this time with more confidence, in better shape, and with a new outlook. MY WORST NIGHTMARE HAD A PURPOSE. It was the answer to my prayers in disguise. Vancouver was my springboard for All-Star appearances, World Series Games, and my eventual induction into the Baseball Hall of Fame.

I have always hoped that this event in my life could serve to encourage others. In the very least, it does provide an interesting way of approaching one of life's set-backs--as the possibility of being the best thing that could have happened!!

Sincerely yours,

Brooks Robinson

"Miracles do not happen
in contradiction to
nature, but only in
contradiction to that
which is known to us of
nature."

– Saint Augustine

DEXTER YAGER

BUSINESSMAN/ ENTREPRENEUR

...is shown here with his wife, Birdie. Both are best-selling authors and millionaires many times over. Their influence has touched the lives of hundreds of thousands worldwide through their Network Marketing business.

Dexter and Birdie Yager are among the most impressive people I have ever met in my life. Dexter, with his winning smile, and Birdie, with her gentle demeanor are quite obviously devoted to each other. They are also devoted to sharing a dream.

Dexter's dreams have elevated him from near poverty to become one of America's most influential and wealthy leaders. He is one of the few, I might add, who is willing to share his knowledge and experience openly. Dexter Yager is truly committed to helping others. I have seen him freely giving his time to a handful of people; and I have watched tens of thousands hanging onto his every word.

The list of senators, celebrities, and world leaders who return Dexter's phone calls is a very long list indeed. And yet, for a man with wealth and power at his fingertips, he is incredibly modest. The only reason that Dexter finds for pointing to himself...is to encourage someone else. "If I can achieve success," he says, "then so can you!"

If it is a good thing to feed a man, it is infinitely better to teach him to feed himself. Dexter believes in this concept, and he is teaching hundreds of thousands of people. They, in turn, will teach millions. Dexter Yager is sharing his dream!

D & B

Yager Enterprises, Incorporated

12201 Steele Creek Road • P.O. Box 412080 • Charlotte, NC 28241-8834

Andy Andrews
P.O. Box 2761
Gulf Shores, AL 36542

Dear Andy,

When I was about 10 years old, a young female playmate told me I would never be anything unless I would go to Catholic school and become a Catholic like she was. Throughout my school years I was constantly told by many teachers that I would never amount to anything unless I went to college. Several kids in school treated me as though I was dumb in certain areas and would never succeed.

When I began my Amway business, many people I talked to about the Amway business laughed at me and said I'd never make it. A neighbor who was a military officer told me even if I succeeded, who would want to know me because of my limited ability of the English language. Several people in Amway told me I was in the wrong line of sponsorship and I couldn't succeed. The first book I wrote, Don't Let Anybody Steal Your Dream was rejected by many publishers and I therefore had to publish it myself. In 1986, following a stroke that paralyzed my entire right side, several doctors told me I'd be confined to a wheelchair for the rest of my life.

Every time these people would tell me these types of things it would hurt me tremendously, but I'd smile and try to ignore the hurt. I would always pray about it all, but under my breath I would say to myself..."you'll eat those words."

When my wife and I were dating, her doctors told her due to medical complications, she'd never be able to have children. These are only a few of the challenges that come to mind over the years.

Well, I never became a Catholic or went to Catholic school, I barely graduated from high school and never attended college. In fact, most summers I ended up taking history and English to pass the previous year.

I've always dreamed big and loved to hear the stories of others' successes. That would give me hope. I read the Bible and that gave me faith and ability. I've met the last five U.S. Presidents personally on several occasions, and been to the White House many of those times.

I've known personally many famous entertainers, movie stars and other celebrities. I've now written nine books. My first book, Don't Let Anybody Steal Your Dream, has now sold more than one-million copies. My wife and I have seven children and now ten grandchildren. I have built one of the largest distributorships in the world of Amway, and speak to several hundred thousands of people every year.

After much hard work and lots of prayer, I walk now without the use of a wheelchair or a cane. Most people would never believe the crippleness my body has gone through. I have a slight limp now and had to become left-handed at the age of 47 after being right-handed all my life. When I was 40 years old, because of high blood pressure, a doctor told me I wouldn't see the age of 50. December 6, 1990 I'll be 51. I continue to lead an active life and still continually reach for new goals and accomplishments.

Tyndale House Publishers, a well known publisher worldwide, is presently publishing my book. This is the third joint venture with them and just recently we received the word that B.Dalton and Waldenbooks has placed orders for my latest book.

Andy, I appreciate the opportunity and honor to be requested to be a part of this book.

Best regards,

Dexter R. Yager

"Our doubts are traitors,
and make us lose the
good we oft might win,
by fearing to attempt."

– William Shakespeare
Measure For Measure

SHIRLEY MULDOWNEY

DRAG RACER

*...divides her time
between homes in
Michigan and Southern
California. She
maintains a full schedule
of racing and public
appearances.*

    I contacted Shirley Muldowney through a series of friends and friends of friends. She was immediately open to the idea of writing a letter and, in fact, told me part of her story that day over the phone.

    I was impressed by her lack of bitterness at the time spent in her career fighting just to compete. She laughingly commented on the irony of having persevered, obtaining a woman's right to race, and now having more competition because of it!

    Drag racing has become even more high-tech since Shirley began. The engines are more powerful, there are more drivers involved, and the financial stakes are greater. But Shirley has maintained an increasingly high profile in a sport where name recognition means sponsorships. Her skill is a matter of record, and in the world of Formula One Drag Racing, the "first lady" will always be Shirley Muldowney.

23340 SHEPHERD LANE
MT. CLEMENS, MICHIGAN 48045

Mr. Andy Andrews
P.O. Box 2761
Gulf Shores, Alabama 36547

Dear Andy:

Have you seen the puzzles that ask the question: what doesn't belong in this picture? Well, in the early part of my career the answer would have been Shirley Muldowney. As a woman in a totally male dominated sport, I was resisted and rejected by virtually everyone involved. The drivers and crews didn't want to race against me and a sponsorship at that time seemed impossible. Even the governing body of the sport, The National Hot Rod Association, tried to prevent me from racing by going so far as to declare my license invalid.

You know, looking back, it was tough to hang in there while seemingly everyone was against my dream, but I managed to do just that. I wrote letters, I hired lawyers, I fought and yelled.

Slowly, things turned around. My attitude and persistence was noticed by other drivers and I began to be accepted. Not too long after that, I signed my first sponsor, Amalie Oil came aboard for $500.

Why didn't I quit? I could have, you know, and no one would have blamed me. I was in uncharted territory; doing something no other woman had ever done. I didn't quit because I wanted it badly enough. I loved driving the car! It was and continues to be my dream. Always remember, the value of persistence is in the fact that so few people have any, you'll be left at the finish line when everyone else has quit in the middle of the race!

Because of my persistence, I was the first woman to feel the power of a 4,000 horsepower engine. I know what it is like to drive a quarter-mile in 4.96 seconds--careening down the track at 289 miles per hour. I am living proof of what a "never say die" attitude can do.

Let me close with the encouragement to believe in your own dreams. Don't buy into the expectations others may have for you. Not a day goes by that I don't remember a quote from one of my high school teachers. "You know, Shirley," she said, "you're not going to make your living riding around in fast cars!"

Chase your dreams,

Shirley Muldowney

JACK HANNA

ZOO DIRECTOR

...one of the most recognized animal experts in America today, he is currently the Executive Director of the Columbus Zoo in Columbus, Ohio.

The first time I saw Jack Hanna, he made me laugh. He was putting a roach on David Letterman. The first time I met Jack Hanna, he made me perspire. He was putting a roach on me. It was a Giant Madagascar Hissing Roach. It was really big, it really hissed, and I still get the creeps just thinking about it!

I was doing a "Special" for The Nashville Network that day. Jack let me hold a baby gorilla, pat an elephant's tongue, and feed white tiger cubs, but after more than a year, people still ask about the roaches. Be careful if you are fortunate enough to meet Jack. He quite often carries three or four of the ugly things around with him. Seriously! They are in a small zip-up bag in his pocket. The man can be a lot of fun out in public!

Jack presently makes regular appearances on "Late Night With David Letterman" and "Good Morning America." He can also be found roaming the grounds of the Columbus Zoo, greeting visitors, and, I hope, gathering anecdotes for a sequel to his best-selling book, *MONKEYS ON THE INTERSTATE*.

Mr. Andy Andrews
P.O. Box 2761
Gulf Shores, Alabama   36542

Dear Andy,

What a challenge you've presented! Normally, life just goes on from one
day to the next, overlapping, and we don't stop to isolate events. But I'll
try.

First of all, what you see is what you get with me. I'm what and who I am.
No pretenses. I'm energetic (hyperactive, some say). A clean desk person.
I read magazines and newspapers--few books. Watch little television. I work
hard and have always been enthusiastic. It's always been that way.

Even as a youngster, I always wanted to be involved with animals. This desire
got me in no end of hot water in high school and college, and became the
driving force of my adult career. It has brought me satisfaction, adventure
throughout the world, and a fair share of criticism.

I've needed to call on some of the above qualities a couple of times in my
life. The first time, I was 25, a new father, and just starting a new pet
shop in Knoxville, my home town. Disaster struck when a woman asked to take
her three-year-old son out to visit the exotic animals I kept at my farm.
The next thing I knew, a 300-lb lioness had torn off the child's arm. This
was your worst nightmare come true. A child's life was in ruins, and I was
responsible. Not only were two families' lives shattered, but the public
castigation was terrible. I don't normally run away from my problems, but
we were a young family with two small daughters to consider. We left
Knoxville to start over in Georgia.

Three years and another daughter later found us returning to Knoxville from
Georgia via Florida, where I had worked at an exotic animal holding facility,
been the director of a small zoo, and dabbled in the wildlife movie business.
We were literally in the middle of unpacking when Julie, our two year old,
was diagnosed as suffering from leukemia. I'd had my career and financial
setbacks, but we had always managed with good humor and optimism. The next
few months were hell, though, with Julie receiving treatment in isolation
and my wildlife career at a dead end as I sold real estate.

Accredited Member American Association Zoological Parks and Aquariums

Julie finally was in remission, so that nightmare at least was on hold. Then, as often happens, friends come through when times are bad. A friend called me with word that the Columbus Zoo directorship was available...in a city with a fine Children's Hospital.

But friends can't always create miracles. I'm a controversial sort of guy in the zoo world. I'm not a vet or a scientist or an accountant. My talent is promotion, and some of my peers are offended at the way I go about selling the Columbus Zoo and conservation. I say what I think and don't always follow the traditional model. I almost got taken behind the woodshed by the American Association of Zoological Parks and Aquariums ethics committee when I strung a tightrope across the tiger yard and had one of the Wallendas walk on it. I admit I went too far on that one, but we did have great attendance that day.

If I sometimes do first and think later, if I sometimes speak out when I should keep my mouth shut, if I sometimes damn the torpedoes--full speed ahead, its because I am who I am. I can face the benefits and the consequences of this because I am doing the work I love, promoting the welfare of animals and turning people on to conservation.

Andy, I know this letter isn't exactly about rejection, but the first two events were great influences in my life, and the last story tells you something about me. Writing this letter has brought back good and bad memories. Thanks for asking!

Sincerely,

Jack Hanna
Executive Director

"Coincidence is God's
way of performing
miracles anonymously."

– Anonymous

CHARLEY PRIDE

ENTERTAINER

...has thirty-nine gold albums, two platinum albums, and one quadruple platinum. He has been awarded three Grammys and has twice been named the Country Music Association's Entertainer of the Year.

Charley Pride is one of country music's most valued recording artists. As is evidenced by his string of gold albums and many awards, he was obviously destined to become a performer. It is interesting to note, however, that music was not his first choice. It is also interesting to note that every time I thought I knew what a person would write about in their letter, I was wrong!

Charley has told stories of walking onstage early in his career to audiences who had no idea he was black. They had only heard his records. I have listened to tapes of some of those shows and it is clear that with his humor and genuine love for people, Charley was an immediate hit. Even today, his attitude about that time in his life is one of amusement. On national television one night, I told Charley that he had truly changed the complexion of country music. He laughed harder than anyone else!

Today, Charley lives and works out of the Dallas/Ft. Worth area. Rozene, his wife of almost thirty years, is active in his business affairs and quite often accompanies him on tours to Canada, Europe, and Australia where, believe it or not, Charley Pride is an even bigger star.

Mr. Andy Andrews
P.O. Box 2761
Gulf Shore, Alabama 36547

Hello Andy,

No one has ever asked me to write about my failures
without my success. My biggest disappointment in life
was not in music, it was in baseball. I wanted to be the
biggest name in major league baseball and then try my luck
with singing. I left home at the age of 16 to pursue my
baseball career. I played on several minor league clubs.
I worked and saved my money to go to spring training,
hoping I would make the major leagues.

In 1961 I went to Palm Springs, CA to try out with the
Angels and try to make the club. I tried too hard and
hurt my arm. Marv Grisson was the pitching coach. After
about a week he came to me and advised me that I did not
have a major league arm, so they would have to let me go.
I went to Mr. Autry, the owner, and asked him not to let
them send me home. He said that he had nothing to do with
the ball club. He said that Bill Rigney, Fred Haney and
Marv Grisson were the ones that decided when and where.
So I was sent home with a tuna fish sandwich and an
orange. Later Gene Autry said that was the best thing he
could have done for me.

The following year I went to spring training with the Mets
in St. Petersburg, Fl. Casey Stengel was the manager
then. I had sent my autographed bats on ahead of my
arrival. It appeared that I was going go get looked at.
After a while and discussions with Tom Johnson, who was
the minor league organization's administrator, he said
they were not going to look at me. So Casey Stengel said,
"we are not running a try out camp down here, take him
out in one of those pastures and look at him". That was
about it for my baseball career. For a long time this had
been my dream and needless to say the disappointment was
great.

After I left St. Petersburg, even though I was
disappointed, I decided to try something else. However,
to this day I have not given up the thought of playing
baseball. I still feel I could have played. Who knows, I
may still give it a try.

Sincerely,

Charley Pride
Charley Pride

BART STARR

FORMER NFL QUARTERBACK

...named the Most Valuable Player in Super Bowl I and II. He was chosen as Player of the Decade in 1970 and was inducted into the Pro Football Hall of Fame in 1977.

The first time we met, I was sitting across from Bart and Cherry Starr on an American Airlines flight. I had been enjoying the parade of men asking Bart to autograph something "for my son." He did so, with a smile, every time. He is unfailingly cordial and polite--and still the only person I have ever seen apologize to a flight attendant for talking during the safety instructions!

As one might imagine, I was thrilled to receive a letter from Bart for this book. His story of dedication and persistence is an encouraging example of his approach to tough times. Not very long ago, however, Bart and Cherry experienced a nightmare of epic proportions--the death of a son due to a drug problem.

This is a horrible situation under any circumstance, but when it happens in a family such as the Starrs, the media scrutiny and public curiosity can be excruciating. Bart and Cherry, however, after a period of reflection and a gathering of thoughts, have turned even the death of their own son into a way of helping others. Both are involved and deeply committed to the reality of a Drug Free America. They travel extensively, making public appearances and speaking to young people and parents alike about the dangers of drugs. They are a couple coming through a storm of their own...and working to bring about a perfection in the lives of others.

STARR SANDERS PROPERTIES

Mr. Andy Andrews
P.O. Box 2761
Gulf Shores, AL   36547

Dear Andy:

What a wonderful idea to have people from so many walks of life share their difficulties and disappointments on their way to success. May your book serve as an inspiration to all those who are facing adversity and choose not to give up the struggle. The rewards will be well worth their efforts.

The 1956 N.F.L. Draft was down to the last few rounds and my dreams of becoming a pro quarterback were quickly fading. It had been hours and the draft was almost over.

The anxiety and disappointment were overwhelming. Because I had been hurt most of my senior year at the University of Alabama, I did not anticipate being selected early but surely someone saw I performed well before I was sidelined with a back injury.

Every name player in the country had been chosen, it seemed, and my name had not come up. Upset, I walked out of the room and then the phone rang. Cherry answered. It was for me. The Green Bay Packers had made me their choice in the 17th round. I was so happy I would have signed for practically nothing - in fact I did - $6,500!

Making the team would be the toughest challenge I had ever faced. I would be competing against 4 other name QB's but I wanted this more than anything in the world and I would be ready.

I spent weeks before my first training camp getting in shape and refining my passing skills. I must have thrown thousands of balls through an old tire hung from an "A" frame at my in-laws home. As my arm grew stronger Cherry joked that the best part of the routine was the seven pounds she lost retrieving all those balls for me.

I reported to camp in July - ready but scared to death. It soon became obvious the Packers did not expect me to stay long. When jerseys were given out for our first photo session, they didn't give me a QB's number. My rookie football cards today show me wearing #42!

Training camp was tough and the competition fierce but the early preparation was paying off, along with the extra hours spent every evening studying my playbook. When I went on the field each day, I felt better prepared and more confident than the previous day.

That confidence enabled me to perform well in scrimmages and pre-season games until, following the final squad reduction, I was given a new jersey, number 15. There are only a few times when I was more excited.

The Packers struggled through 3 dismal years (1956-1958) under two different coaching staffs and morale was low. In a bold move, a little known assistant coach, Vince Lombardi was hired to coach the Packers in 1959.

If I thought making the team was tough my rookie year, proving myself to Lombardi was even tougher. My quiet manner did not impress him but my work habits and stability did. However, he still felt I was only good enough to be his back-up quarterback. I prepared each week as though I were going to start so when our QB went down with an injury in a big game I was ready. This was what I had worked so hard for. I had to prove to Lombardi I was the best man for this job.

We came from behind to win and I was now the starting QB for the Green Bay Packers. We were 7-5 that year and on our way to one of the most exciting eras in pro football.

I spent 16 years with the Green Bay Packers playing for one of the greatest coaches in football history. The Packers' success under Vince Lombardi is legendary (five championships and two Super Bowls during a seven year span) and I am proud to be part of that history.

Sincerely,

Bart

Bart Starr

BS/aaa

324 North 21st Street Birmingham, Alabama 35203 • Phone 205/328-0400 • FAX 205/326-0919

"For He will command
His angels concerning
you to guard you in all
your ways; they will lift
you up in their hands, so
that you will not strike
your foot against a
stone."

– Psalms 91:11,12

JAMESON PARKER

ACTOR

...is best known for his work on the television series "Simon and Simon" and the daytime drama "One Life To Live." He has also made sixteen feature films and television movies.

"Simon And Simon" ran for eight years on CBS and during that time, Jameson Parker became known to the nation. He had already achieved a large measure of success playing the part of a villain in a daytime drama, but this was different. This was prime-time. Millions of people were watching and, with Gerald McRaney as his brother Rick, Jameson was the star of the show.

With that stardom came an opportunity that Jameson embraced with open arms. He had a chance to make a difference in other people's lives. He became heavily involved in fund raising for charitable causes, conservation efforts, and in many ways encouraging those he saw who were less fortunate than himself.

I met Jameson at a celebrity event for WATERFOWL USA in Texas. We talked and as I told him about this book, he smiled and assured me that, yes, he would write a letter. It was waiting for me when I got home, three days later.

Since the average letter in this book took several months to receive, I was curious about the motivation for his promptness. And later, after we had become friends, I found out.

Jameson has a beautiful, four year old daughter named Katherine who has Muscular Dystrophy. Besides the work he does for the Muscular Dystrophy Association, Jameson actively searches for ways to inspire the victims of this disease.

"If my words embolden the spirit of just one child," he says, "then the time I spent committing them to paper has been worthwhile."

JAMESON PARKER

Dear Andy,

    Diana McBriar refused to go out with me in college and since it was in college that I decided to become an actor, you could say that her rejection set the stage for a lifetime of rejections that continues to this day. You see, an actor's life is synonymous with rejection. For every hundred scripts you read, you get turned down ninety-nine times, and it doesn't matter what they say ["You're not right for this part." "You're too young for this part." "You're too old." "You're too short." "You're too tall." "You're too blond." "You're not blond enough."] what you hear is: "YOU AREN'T GOOD ENOUGH!" Since actors are pretty insecure anyway, this constant rejection can make it awfully difficult to press on.

    One particularly brutal rejection early in my career stands out in my memory as an example of what actors go through. By way of giving some background to put this anecdote in perspective let me point out that I was thrown out of two boarding schools, suspended from college [and turned down by Diana McBriar!] rejected by the Army for a physical disability [and they were desperate for men at that time] and on top of everything else I had a slight learning disability which, since it hadn't ever been properly diagnosed, left me convinced that I was stupid. All in all, I was at pretty low ebb.

    Anyway, I had just moved to New York and was so green I still had manure on my boots. A successful friend took pity on me and arranged an interview with a Very Important Agent at a Very Famous Agency. Full of hope and clutching my picture and resume [a work of semi-fiction] I arrived at the appointed hour and was told by an extremely bored receptionist to take a seat and wait. And I waited. Cobwebs were hanging off me by the time I was finally summoned. I made my way down a labyrinth of corridors and finally into a lavish office where an elegant and immaculate lady sat reading behind a desk. Without looking up she held up one hand, indicating that I should wait. Well, I was getting good at that. I waited. Finally, still without looking up, she said,

"Picture," and I slid my picture across the vast expanse of her desk. She glanced briefly at it and at my poor little resume on the back, slid them back to me and looked up at me for the first time. I have now, mercifully, forgotten her exact words, but, oh, I will never forget their content. She said, in essence, "I've seen twenty like you today. They were all better looking and they were better actors. Go back to Virginia." Well, I crept out under the door. But after awhile a curious thing happened. I got angry and my anger turned to rage and my rage crystallized into determination. I made up my mind I was going to make it in the business if it killed me! I hadn't yet read Calvin Coolidge's famous statement:

> "Nothing in the world can take the
> place of persistence. Talent will
> not; nothing is more common than
> unsuccessful men with talent.
> Genius will not; unrewarded genius
> is almost a proverb. Education
> will not; the world is full of
> educated derelicts. Persistence and
> determination alone are omnipotent."

If I had, I would have had those words tatooed across my chest!

Well, I've been persistent, and while I still get rejected more often than not, I just keep plugging away. I wonder whatever happened to Diana McBriar?

Sincerely,

Jameson Parker

Jameson Parker

"Nothing great was ever
achieved without
enthusiasm."

– *Emerson*

TOM GALLA

LITTLE LEAGUE BASEBALL COACH

...is a partner in the Insurance Agency of Curtiss, Crandon, and Moffette, Inc. On summer afternoons, he can still be found working with young people in Trumbull, Connecticut as a baseball coach.

I started playing Little League the summer I turned eleven. We had green caps with a big "B" on the front. Blumberg's Department Store was our sponsor. We weren't a great team, but it really didn't seem to matter. Our coach was constantly stressing good sportsmanship and teamwork. He taught us the fundamentals. He showed us how to bunt...and showed us how to laugh at ourselves--when *he* tripped over home plate. He was a great guy. We learned a lot and had a blast.

Tom Galla seems to be the same kind of coach. He knows instinctively which kids need him to be a stern disciplinarian and which ones need his arm around their shoulder. He is a master at encouraging young people and calming their fears. It is a special talent that few men take time to develop.

Tom began coaching several years ago--teaching the young people in his care about working for goals and reaching for the stars. Then, in the summer of 1989, he took a group of eleven and twelve year olds from a small town in the Northeast--and turned them into World Champions.

Trumbull Little League
P.O. Box 145
Trumbull, Connecticut 06611
Home of the 1989 World Series Champions

Mr. Andy Andrews
P.O. Box 2761
Gulf Shores, Alabama   36542

Dear Andy,

Oh, you've brought back such wonderful memories with your call. To say that being the manager of a World Champion Little League team is the most exciting thing to ever happen to me is an understatement. I've got to tell you honestly, however, that I never in a minute believed it could really happen. I dreamt that it could, but cold hard facts told me that it would be nearly impossible. First of all, there were 7,000 teams involved in the largest round robin tournament ever held in any sport. Secondly, every step of the way becomes more difficult and in spite of terrific talent, there could always be a team ready to beat you on any given day. And, last but not least, Taiwan was nearly always the final opponent and they don't visit the U.S.A. to return home as runners-up.

Back on August 1, 1989, Trumbull National was defeated 2-0 by Park City American (from Bridgeport, Conn.) in our local district tourna- ment. This tournament is the first obstacle that we needed to overcome on our long road to Williamsport. Luckily, this was a double elimination tournament and we were able to bounce back and defeat that same team 7-0 two days later. This was our only loss along the way and I believe it taught us a very valuable lesson. Up until this point we had played four games and outscored our opponents 85-8 and I believe that things were going a little too easily. By losing, the players and coaches were awa- kened to realize that it could be over at any time and to any opponent. We were all having too much fun to let it end, so we became more deter- mined and focused on what we wanted to achieve. From the beginning we told the boys that Williamsport was our goal and we had as much chance as any other team to get there. And I believed it!

We had <u>hard work</u>, <u>dedication</u>, <u>team chemistry</u>, <u>good luck</u>, and <u>talent</u> of the players and this all paid off game after game as we got closer to our goal. The Eastern Regionals were scary in that we had to play and win all four of our scheduled games in a period of five days. We outscored our opponents 51-14 which seems to indicate an easy time, but believe me it never felt easy. In our second game against Manchester, New Hampshire we won by a score of 1-0 in one of the best pitching and defensive games I've ever seen. This game was reinforcing the lesson we had learned against Park City way back on August 1st.

So, it was off to the "mecca" of Little League baseball on August 20, 1989 for a dream come true. We were such a different team now than we had been back on July 15th when the team first came together. The boys were no longer unsure of their abilities. They no longer took anyone else for granted and they played each game with all the intensity they had. But Andy, let me tell you, when we arrived and saw the beautiful stadium and then met the Taiwanese team face to face we all were reduced to a bunch of "wide-eyed" kids again wondering what in the world we were doing there. There was a choice to be made. We could be satisfied with our tremendous success and enjoy the week by swimming in the large pool located in our complex or we could go back to basics and work hard to try to win it all. There was no choice as we were committed to being the best we could be.

Our first practice was scheduled for one hour after arrival. It was the toughest practice that we had ever held. But the biggest change was made in our mental attitude toward where we were and what we were trying to accomplish. The hard workout focused us back on the job at hand and that was simply to win one game at a time. Davenport, Iowa was our first opponent so there was no need to worry about Taiwan, at least not yet. That game, if it ever happened, was light years away. Andy, it worked because the boys played like men that week. They defeated Iowa and then San Pedro, California in two close, hard-fought games and believe it or not we were going to play Kaohsiung, Taiwan on August 26, 1989 for the World Championship. It was almost anti-climactic in that we had come so far and overcome so many obstacles to arrive there. But you know what, we decided that we were one of two teams that would be taking the field on that final day of Little League play in 1989 and only one team could win. And, why shouldn't that team be Trumbull!

Andy, the fact that we did beat Taiwan that day by a score of 5-2 makes me very proud but does not surprise me. That's what we had prepared for. What made me so proud was the fact that our boys (12 year old men) were able to stand up to the pressure and play the game beautifully, the way it should be played, in front of 40,000+ fans and millions on national television.

Whether we had won or lost that final game Trumbull had proven that hard work, dedication, talent and lots of good old-fashioned luck could make it possible for anyone to fulfill their dreams.

Sincerely,

Tom Galla, Manager
1989 Little League
World Champions

"If you have faith as a
mustard seed, you will
say to this mountain,
'Move...' and nothing will
be impossible."

— Matthew 17:20

PHOTO BY EIKA AOSHIMA

AMY GRANT

ENTERTAINER

...is a five time Grammy award winner. She has recorded seven gold and six platinum albums.

Amy Grant has the kind of voice that can only be described as an instrument. Her first album was released when she was only a teenager, but even then, she had a mature, rich sound.

Contemporary Christian recordings had been her main focus for years. Only recently has a gradual shift in Amy's style and music been revealed. By remaining true in spirit and in her approach to live performances, Amy has enjoyed the public's approval and support of this change in career direction.

Through her recordings, videos, and live concerts, Amy Grant has touched millions of people. Children and adults alike are charmed by her wonderful voice and good natured humor. The effort she put forth early in her career learning to ignore rejection was worth it...for all of us.

Amy Grant

Dear Andy,

Back in the Spring of 1978 I released my first album. I was seventeen years old and full of dreams. That summer, after my class graduated from high school, I left on my first promotional tour. One stop on that tour was a book and record store in Southern California. I was to sign autographs and sing for ninety minutes. My mother was with me and we were very excited. The manager of the store had sent out 1200 engraved invitations for the occasion. Obviously, everyone involved was expecting a large crowd.

Well, the crowd never made it. In fact, not one single person showed up! How can a store stay in business with no walk-up shoppers? Oh well - the store manager listened to me sing for an hour and a half. He listened to me sing by himself because even my mother left. (I'm not kidding!) This probably still ranks as the single most "distinguishing" event of my career.

I can't say, without a doubt, that quitting didn't enter my mind that day, but I'm glad that I didn't. That experience (and several like it) gave me a deep appreciation for the support of a kind audience that I might never have gained otherwise. Besides, the memory of that afternoon still makes me laugh inside, just as I did the last time I looked out from the stage of the Pacific Amphitheater in Southern California to 20,000 smiling faces.

I know that there are no guarantees in life. I also know that good things rarely come about the first time around. And so my advice to anyone reading this letter would be: whatever your goals - don't give up! More important than talent, strength, or knowledge is the ability to laugh at yourself and enjoy the pursuit of your dreams.

Sincerely,

Amy Grant

P.O. Box 25330 • Nashville, Tennessee 37202-5330

BOB HOPE

ENTERTAINER

...starred in fifty-six movies and over 500 Bob Hope Specials. He has been entertaining American military personnel all over the world since 1941.

Not too long ago, at a benefit concert, I was about to walk onstage. Suddenly, the promoter of the event rushed up and said the seven most terrifying words I have ever heard in my life: "BOB HOPE IS IN THE FIRST ROW!" I looked, and sure enough, he was there--the same guy I had watched for years. I rarely get very nervous before a show, but that night I almost passed out!

Everyone has heroes. One of mine just happens to be Bob Hope. His commitment to our country, the tireless schedule he keeps, and the continuing freshness of his comedy are only a few of the things I admire about this man.

After the show, I met him in the hall backstage and for a brief time, we talked. He modestly brushed aside the compliments I was trying to heap upon him. Instead, he asked about specific routines I had done and wanted to know how my golf game was. "Non-existent," I told him.

Since that night, I have talked with Mr. Hope on several occasions. A few times by phone and, recently, with him by the pool in his back yard. I am still strangely nervous around him, but through no fault of his. He is friendly, polite, and genuinely funny. It's just that he's...well, he's Bob Hope!

BOB HOPE

Andy Andrews
Post Office Box 2761
Gulf Shores, AL   36547

Dear Andy,

You know I've been awfully lucky these last
50 years in show business, but I had my
other tough moments. For instance...

Around 1928, I went into Evansville, Indiana
to do an act. I was having some breakfast
so I looked at the paper to see what kind of
billing I had at the theatre and it said,
Ben Hope! So I took the paper and I rushed
into the theatre. I said to the manager,
"What's the idea of spelling my name that
way?" He said, "What name?" I said, "Ben Hope!,
What kind of thing is that?" He said, "Well,
what is your name?" I said, "Bob Hope" and
he said, "Well who knows?". I guess at that
time nobody knew and nobody cared, but I got
a pretty good break because at least I was
working a few places.

Now about six months before that, I was standing
in front of the Woods Theatre Building in
Chicago. I had been getting ten dollars a show,
but I couldn't even get that. Nobody knew me.
My name was Lester Hope so I decided to change
it to Bob Hope cause it sounded more chummy,
but I still starved. I couldn't get a date,
I wasn't eating very well and my laundry was
piling up. I was just about ready to go home
to Cleveland to get a full meal and my laundry
cleaned, when this friend of mine walked up.

He was a very successful Vaudevillian, Charlie
Cooley, and he said, "How you doing?" I said,
"I'm starving." He said, "Come with me" and
took me up and introduced me to Charlie Hogan his
booker. He booked small theatres in and around
Chicago. He said, "I can give you one day at
the West Inglewood Theatre, will twenty-five
dollars be all right?" Well I gulped, because
I'd only been making ten a show at that time.
That was the date that got me rolling.

Andy, we all have our slack moments and they're
interesting to look back on. It sort of levels
you off a little bit.

I'll see you down in Port Arthur.
                    Good luck,

                    Bob

THOMAS S. MONAGHAN

ENTREPRENEUR

...is the founder of Domino's Pizza, Inc. He now owns the Detroit Tigers baseball team and is actively involved in the support of charitable causes.

Tom Monaghan is a man who has helped most of us many times. Not directly, of course, but by having his pizzas delivered...hot and on time! When he conceived the idea of guaranteeing delivery in thirty minutes or less, there were those in the business world who said it would never work. As we all know, it did work, and a very nice man became a mega-success.

There are very few towns in this country without a Domino's. Most have more than one. The enormous popularity of these pizzas has enabled Mr. Monaghan to indulge his dreams. He has his own professional baseball team and is now able to support his church not only with his time, but in a financially substantial way.

When I received his letter, I was interested in Mr. Monaghan's comments concerning failure. "A failure," he says, "is when you stop trying, and I never did that."

Neither did I. I was turned down two times by office personnel before my third request for a letter from Mr. Monaghan was accepted. I can only believe that the first two never saw his desk!

Thanks for your letter, Sir. I'm glad I didn't give up!

Domino's Pizza, Inc.
30 Frank Lloyd Wright Drive
P.O. Box 997
Ann Arbor, Michigan 48106-0997

Mr. Andy Andrews
P.O. Box 2761
Gulf Shores, AL 36547

Dear Mr. Andrews:

Thank you for the invitation to contribute to your book to help encourage others to overcome obstacles and achieve their goals.

Obstacles, I certainly know all about those. When I started Domino's Pizza in 1960, I had no idea what was in store for me. After a childhood of living in orphanages and detention homes I struggled to fund my college education with hopes of becoming an architect.

As a means to do this, I purchased a pizza store in Ypsilanti with my brother Jim. The store turned into a full time job, causing me to make the decision to not enroll the next semester at school and stick to the pizza business.

When my pizza store earned a reputation as being the best in the area and sales were increasing, I started to expand with more outlets. The financial setbacks and disagreements with among partners, disolved partnership, and an office fire, a trademark lawsuit appeal all tried our patience tremendously. All of these setbacks I feel, were tools for me to learn from and I used them as stepping stones, and didn't see them as failures. A failure is when you stop trying, and I never did that.

It is safe to say that my life was full of setbacks and rejection, but certainly not failure. If I did not learn from my many mistakes, then I could call them failures, but they were constructive aspects of my life.

Today, looking back at the 30 years since I started Domino's Pizza. I can safely say that 20 of them were one rejection and obstacle after another. In building Domino's Pizza, it has afforded me the resources to greater use in the church, as this work is most important to me. Many of the obstacles I encountered enabled me to see that there are much bigger things than Domino's Pizza, I intend to go after them, and I am prepared for the obstacles this time.

Sincerely,

DOMINO'S PIZZA, INC.

Thomas S. Monaghan
Chairman of the Board

TSM/mm

PHOTO BY PAUL ROBERTSON

GUY HUNT

GOVERNOR

...is a former cattle farmer now serving his second term as Governor of the State of Alabama.

Governor Guy Hunt is a physically imposing man. He is extremely tall and has an air of seriousness about him. He is a conservative Republican in a state where Democrats traditionally rule the roost. When he started his campaign for the governor's office in 1986, Hunt was dismissed as a possible winner by every major newspaper in the state.

Being from Alabama, I followed the campaign and election with great interest. The fact that he continued to work on in the face of tremendous odds intrigued me. The fact that he actually won was absolutely inspirational.

I have, in the past two years, been privileged to spend some time with Governor and Mrs. Hunt. I have seen first hand the compassion he has for the people in his state. I have also been witness to his wonderful sense of humor--he's not nearly so imposing as a first glance would have one believe! And I've seen the spirit that enables him to work as though everything depends on him...and pray as if nothing does.

STATE OF ALABAMA

GOVERNOR'S OFFICE

MONTGOMERY 36130

GUY HUNT
GOVERNOR

Mr. Andy Andrews
P.O. Box 2761
Gulf Shores, Alabama 36547

Dear Andy:

As a child I learned from my father to work hard and take pride in everything I did. Growing up on a farm in rural Alabama was indeed a challenge. Life was not easy, but it was my goal to one day make Alabama the very best state in which to live.

Becoming governor is not something I accomplished overnight. As a young adult, I saw that there were things in government that I thought could be done differently and better. The first office I ran for was that of State Senator. This was my first political defeat, but it was not my last attempt to hold office. I ran for Cullman County Probate Judge and won in 1964.

In 1978, I sought the office of governor, lost, regrouped, ran again and won in 1986. But it was during the 1986 campaign that I personally was rejected by a small group of the electorate, who also happened to be my peers.

I have been a farmer and cattleman all of my life. During the 1986 campaign, the Alabama Cattlemen's Association planned their annual governor's luncheon for all the major gubernatorial candidates. A friend of mine asked me to attend the luncheon, but he later had to withdraw the invitation because "only viable candidates for governor" were invited to speak. Little did they know a few months later I would be sworn in as the first Republican governor of Alabama in 112 years.

It was this type of rejection by my peers which inspired me and my campaign people to work harder. My father long ago taught me an important principle from which I have never shied, and that's to never quit. I believed I could be elected the governor of Alabama if I continued to work in spite of what some groups thought of me.

As you know Andy, there are few things in this life which are given to us. It takes a strong will, determination, support from your family and a belief in God and oneself.

I appreciate the opportunity to share a few of my thoughts with you and hope that my story, along with those of others in your book, will serve as an inspiration for others.

God Bless You,

Guy Hunt
Governor

GH:dc

"It is not the critic who counts; not the man who points out how the strong man stumbled, or where the doer of deeds could have done better. The credit belongs to the man who is actually in the arena; whose face is marred by dust and sweat and blood; who strives valiantly; who errs and comes short again and again; who know the great enthusiasms, the great devotions and spends himself in a worthy cause; who at the best knows in the end the triumph of high achievement; and who at the worst, if he fails, at least fails while daring greatly; so that his place shall never be with those cold and timid souls who know neither victory nor defeat."

–*Theodore Roosevelt*

ADMIRAL ALAN SHEPARD

ASTRONAUT

...a Naval test pilot who manned the first U.S. spaceflight. He became the fifth man to walk on the moon.

In May of 1961, when Alan Shepard was launched into space, he was speeding into the unknown. No one could say, absolutely, what the outcome would be. There were loads of theories, but very few facts. He led the way to new frontiers. He was our first man in space.

Today, a space flight can be accomplished with very little fanfare. Even school children understand the concepts of zero-gravity and oxygen-free environments. A space shuttle flight can blast off with barely a mention on the evening news! But in 1961, for Alan Shepard, the nation was holding its breath.

When he safely returned to Earth, Shepard was hailed a true American hero. He had battled the doubts and fears in his own mind and brought to completion a mission that many had considered a dream.

Several years later, Alan Shepard, fought doubt and fear again. And this time, they threatened his very future.

In his letter, Admiral Shepard tells the story of that fight.

SEVEN FOURTEEN ENTERPRISES INC.

Admiral Alan Shepard
President

Mr. Andy Andrews
P. O. Box 2761
Gulf Shores, Alabama   36547

Dear Andy:

I was surprised to receive your recent letter. The fact
that an average comedian wants to associate, vicariously,
with an outstanding and world-renowned astronaut is not what
surprised me. I can relate to that, Mr. Walter Mitty! But
I am totally taken back by the fact that you have learned,
somehow, that my life has not been a series of one major
success after another. Now that you somehow know that
secret, I will have to confess a "little rain" has fallen in
my life from time to time.

Perhaps the most significant and disappointing setback of my
life occurred when I was at the "peak" of my career as an
astronaut. I made the first US spaceflight in May 1961 and
became a public figure and national hero overnight! It was
a heady experience even for one who had already compiled an
outstanding record as a Naval test pilot.

In 1963 NASA assigned me to command the first two-man Gemini
spacecraft with Tom Stafford as my co-pilot. I was
ecstatic, riding on top of the world. We were a couple of
months into our training cycle when it happened! I got out
of bed one morning with total loss of balance, nausea and a
strange ringing in my left ear. Eventually, I was diagnosed
as having Meniere's Syndrome, not as a result of space
flight but a totally debilitating condition, none the less.

NASA grounded me, assigned another crew and told me I could
stick around in a desk job to see if the situation would
improve. I was devastated – the world's greatest astronaut,
grounded! I tried to adjust, I helped train astronauts,
watched them fly and envied them but became totally
frustrated.

After a couple of years, with no improvement, I thought of
quitting the astronauts corps and giving in to my
frustration. But then I thought that I must prevail
somehow and not give up! I stayed on and trained and kept
ready.

3203 Mercer Road, Suite 200   Houston, Texas 77027   Phone 713 840-8064   Fax 713 840-0036

One day I heard of a doctor who might be able to correct my problem with surgery. I made an appointment, met him and he decided that, although risky, an operation might help. He could see that my strong desire to fly again was a very positive factor.

So, on my own, with an assumed name to preclude publicity, I had the operation. And then came a long 6 to 8 month recuperative period, but I didn't give up. Finally, after several medical tests and almost a year after the operation NASA said I could fly again!

As you know, I was selected then to command Apollo 14, the third moon landing, and I became the fifth of twelve men to walk on the moon! What a great personal victory that was!

Had I not believed in myself, had I not persevered in times of total disappointment, had I not had a strong desire to do what I did best, it might never have happened!

This story had a happy ending and, as I look back today on those times, I can't help but think there must be many similar disappointments in the lives to todays youngsters. And perhaps the story of that extra effort which helped me may inspire and help others to produce that little "extra effort" themselves. And how much more satisfying is an achievement in the face of adversity!

My best wishes, dear friend,

Alan Shepard

Alan B. Shepard, Jr.
Rear Admiral, USN (ret)

ABS:sdh

"If you have built castles
in the air, your work
need not be lost; that is
where they should be.
Now put the foundations
under them."

— Thoreau

PETE BABCOCK

**VICE PRESIDENT/
GENERAL MANAGER-
ATLANTA HAWKS**

*...formerly the President
and General Manager of
the Denver Nuggets, he
currently serves in a
similar position with the
National Basketball
Association's Atlanta
Hawks.*

Okay. The Atlanta Hawks have Spud Webb. He's only 5' 6"
and he can dunk the ball. In fact, a couple of years ago, he won
the Slam Dunk Competition at the NBA All-Star Game.

The Hawks also have Dominique Wilkins, a perennial All-Star
who has been called "the human highlight film." Wilkins has also
won the Slam Dunk Competition a couple of times!

Pete Babcock has a job that a lot of guys would love. As the
General Manager of the Atlanta Hawks, he deals daily with some
of the greatest basketball players in the world. What would it be
like, I wonder, to step out of your office for a break, and toss up a
few free throws with the Hawks' massive center, Moses Malone?
Tough job, right?

Well, yeah. For one thing, if the players don't win, the General
Manager is usually asked to find another place to work! It is his
job to bring together the best group of players he can sign,
coordinate them with the best coaches he can find, and literally
will the whole thing to work.

Pete Babcock is one of the few men who has consistently
achieved a high level of excellence in this demanding position.
What's his secret you ask? He focuses on solutions and pushes the
problems aside.

PETE BABCOCK
Vice President & General Manager

Andy Andrews
P.O. Box 2761
Gulf Shores, AL 36547

Dear Andy:

Although I was a mediocre athlete at the high school and college levels, I still had a dream of someday being in the NBA (professional basketball).

I found the path to pro basketball was filled with many setbacks and strange twists. Starting my career as a freshman basketball coach at the high school level, I found the next step of becoming a varsity coach frustrating as I interviewed and pursued five different coaching positions before I finally was hired six years later.

Due to my frustrations of not being able to obtain a varsity coaching job, I turned to scouting on a volunteer basis for an NBA team and a collegiate scouting service. Through two years of volunteer scouting, doors slowly began to open as I moved into regional scouting positions and finally into a full time assistant coaching position with the San Diego Clippers.

Once I had my opportunity to work in the NBA I certainly wanted to make the most of it. In the past ten years I have had the privilege of fulfilling many roles from coaching, scouting and player personnel, to serving as President/General Manager of the Denver Nuggets and ultimately owning a minority share of the Nuggets franchise.

Looking back, I feel my patience and persistence through volunteer and part-time work helped develop an attitude that you truly can find a way to "live your dream". The years of preparation represented an exciting time in my development with many great memories and a true appreciation what it really takes to achieve long term goals.

Although each rejection was a major disappointment, I always learned something from the process that enabled me to do a better job the next time.

Thank you for the opportunity to share my experience with you as it always helps keep things in proper perspective by reviewing the past.

Sincerely,

Pete Babcock

Pete Babcock

Atlanta Hawks

JOAN RIVERS

ENTERTAINER

...one of the biggest names headlining in Las Vegas. She tours the country playing to sold-out theaters and can be seen weekdays on her nationally syndicated television program, "The Joan Rivers Show."

When people find out that I toured as Joan Rivers' opening act off and on for almost two years, they invariably ask the same question: "What is she really like?" It's a question I don't mind answering. Joan Rivers is one of the nicest, most generous people with whom I have ever had the privilege of working.

This is not a casual observance. Understand that I traveled with her; sometimes for weeks at a time. I was around Joan constantly and never once saw her refuse to sign an autograph. Even when we were in a hurry, she took time to really talk to the people who stopped her. I saw Joan on her knees, backstage after a performance, hugging and laughing with children in wheelchairs...not once or twice, but dozens of times.

And she always had time for me. She encouraged me, she bugged me to get married, and she was constantly watching out for my money. Once, she knocked on my dressing room door and asked if I knew how much hamburgers cost at our hotel. They were $8.95 she told me, and proceeded to march me to her dressing room where she insisted that I take the sandwiches and fruit that had been left for her.

I have more stories about Joan Rivers than this space will allow...and they're all good. I'll always be grateful to Joan. She set a wonderful example of how to treat people.

Andy Andrews
P.O. Box 2761
Gulf Shores, AL 35647

Dear Andy,

You want an example of one rejection in my life? Only <u>one</u> rejection?!!
I'd be lucky to keep this letter to one page! As far back as I can
remember, I wanted a career in show business. And as far back as I can
remember, people were telling me "no."

On December 7, 1958, I walked into The Showbar in Boston. I was to be
paid 125 dollars for the week---two shows a night. I had already checked
into the hotel across the street. It was a dirty, horrible place, but I
didn't care. This was my first job.

I had already been turned down by every agent in New York when I found
Harry Brent. He was the man willing to work with me, mold my act, and
ultimately book me into The Showbar as "Pepper January...Comedy With
Spice!" Things were really looking up...or so I thought. After the first
show, the manager called me over. "Hey, Pepper," he said, "you're fired."

I was devastated. Fired! Fired from my first job! I went back to my
crummy hotel room and collapsed. I literally could not stop crying. I
cried as I stood under the shower in that filthy tub, my feet protected
with socks, the curtain open so that the killer from "Psycho" could not
stab me! Standing in that dirt-blackened tub, I no longer knew whether
the thing inside me struggling to get out was talent or only an
obsession. But I didn't give in.

Soon, I was booked and fired from my second job. Harry Brent also left me
taking the name "Pepper January" with him. "Women comics I can find," he
explained, "but a name like this is hard to come by!" Meanwhile, I was
back to square one.

Let me condense this letter, Andy, by telling you that I tried everything
and called on everyone. Very little worked and everyone said no. My own
mother said, "You have no talent. You're throwing your life away." One
of the most powerful theatrical agents in the business told me, "You're
too old. If you were going to make it, you would have made it by now."
The talent coordinator for the Tonight Show said, "We just don't think
you'd work on TV." The verdict certainly seemed to be in, but I just
couldn't quit.

I had no money. My office was a phone booth in Grand Central Station. I
lived out of one small suitcase and slept in my car while my father
threatened to have me committed to Bellevue. All in all---not an easy
time. It did, however, serve to shape the determination and an inner
strength I have called on in my life many times since.

Even as I write this, it is far easier to recall my successes than the
failures I've experienced. We all tend to forget the tough times.
Children especially, I believe, sometimes see success as a "lucky lottery
ticket" that one chances upon. And that is why I think it important to
note, that in my case, I was thirty-one years old. Thirty-one years of
hearing "no." Thirty-one long years before the acceptance began. And
that even in my darkest moments, I knew instinctively that my unyeilding
drive was my most valuable asset. Perseverance, my dear, will always be
just as important---important as talent.

Never stop believing! Never give up! Never quit! <u>Never</u>.

Most sincerely,

Joan Rivers

CBS Broadcast Center • 524 West 57th Street • New York, NY 10019
(212) 975-5522

TIM DAGGETT

OLYMPIC GOLD MEDALIST

...was virtually unknown outside the world of gymnastics until the 1984 Summer Olympic Games where he scored a perfect "10" on the Horizontal Bar to win a Gold Medal for the United States.

I have always been an avid follower of the Olympics, so it was not unusual that I happened to be watching as Tim Daggett scored his perfect "10" on the Horizontal Bar. I saw him receive the gold medal as The Star Spangled Banner was being played and even managed to catch his Pommel Horse routine four days later for which he won a Bronze.

In his letter, Tim tells of the rejection he experienced as a young gymnast and how it spurred him to greater heights. There was, however, another battle that he fought; this one three years after his Olympic victories.

In 1987, at the World Championships in Rotterdam, Holland, Tim was competing in the Vault. He ran down the runway and hit the board, but he got a little bit crooked in the air. He landed wrong, and upon impact, completely shattered the bones in his left leg, severing an artery and requiring five different operations.

Facing a forced retirement, Tim had to readjust his dreams. He says, "I knew that my success would now come not from medals, but from trying; from facing the struggle and seeing it through to the end, no matter what the outcome."

Tim is now experiencing the success that the struggle has provided. He is in more demand as a motivational speaker today because he talks honestly about overcoming obstacles. And that honesty comes from experience!

TIM DAGGETT

Olympic Gold Medalist
Motivational Speaker

Mr. Andy Andrews
P.O. Box 2761
Gulf Shores, AL 36542

Dear Andy:

I can't agree with you more! So many people we encounter day in and day out look at anyone who has attained any amount of success in their field as leading a "charmed life". *If they only knew!*

When I first sat down to try and figure out what best describes the difficulties and setbacks I had on my road to success, I was overwhelmed. It appears that these problems or obstacles are not one-time chance encounters, but basically are a part of the big equation of life.

Upon further reflection I decided the one obstacle I would discuss here should be before I had any notoriety or any major success.

I began gymnastics when I was nine years old. It quickly became not merely a sport but a passion in my life. Each day and year I yearned for more and strived for greater heights.

After one successful high school year, finishing first in the state of Massachusetts at the high school gymnastics championships in the all-around, I really thought I was something special. I had taken on the best in Massachusetts and won, and now it was time for the U.S.

My father made the decision that I must try out for our Junior National Team. I boarded my first plane flight ever to the Olympic Training Center in Colorado Springs for my first big shot. To say I was nervous is an understatement.

The first day of the trials I was blown away. Kids my own age and younger were doing more difficult skills, better than I'd ever seen before. When it came my turn to compete, I was humiliated. Needless to say, I did not make this Junior National Team. After the trials were over the coaching staff met with each of the participants. Although trying to be compassionate, they felt they had to be honest: Tim Daggett was nowhere near Junior National Team caliber.

"But, Tim, gymnastics can be just for fun, also," one of the coaches told me. I was enraged. We'll see about "fun", I thought. And we'll see about next time.

Instead of feeling sorry for myself I went home and worked harder than I ever had.

143 Rogers Avenue • West Springfield, MA 01089 • 413-733-3609

Two years later I competed in the Junior National Championships alongside all of the participants who had not only made the team two years before in Colorado Springs, but who were so far ahead of me they were out of my league. I finished this competition in 5th place. I made the team.

As I said, this incident was my first rejection, but it certainly was not my last. But even through all the rough times, I feel I came out okay, winning a gold medal in the Olympic Games and various other accomplishments of which I'm equally as proud.

Sincerely,

Tim Daggett

"Difficulties are God's
errands; and when we
are sent upon them, we
should esteem it as a
proof of God's
confidence."

– *Beecher*

STEPHEN J. CANNELL

TELEVISION PRODUCER

...is an Emmy award-winning writer/producer. He is Chairman of the Board and Chief Executive Officer of The Cannell Studios.

Stephen J. Cannell has created or co-created more shows than anyone in the history of television. They include "The Rockford Files," "Baretta," "The A-Team," and "Hunter."

His television career took off in 1966, when he submitted a script for the Universal series "Adam 12." The producers and actors were so impressed by the story line and dialogue that Stephen was immediately asked to serve as head writer! Years of effort had turned him into an "overnight success."

Today, The Cannell Studios has surpassed the one billion dollar production mark and is experiencing remarkable growth and diversification in areas such as comedy, commercials, merchandising, movies, and mini-series. The Cannell Studios recently opened North Shore Studios, which houses Cannell Films of Canada and is Canada's largest full service production facility.

Stephen J. Cannell is providing entertainment for a generation. While reading his letter, it should be remembered that a major factor in his success has been the determination with which he pursued his dreams.

The Cannell Studios

Stephen J. Cannell
CHAIRMAN OF THE BOARD
CHIEF EXECUTIVE OFFICER

Dear Andy,

You asked me to tell you about early failures in my life. Perhaps flunking the first grade is a good place to start. How do you flunk the first grade? It seems that, aside from playing in a sandbox and sitting around being read to by a teacher, there was very little to screw up. This was not, however, the view of my first grade teachers, and I got the ax. Okay, I guess I could survive that. After all, maybe I was six months too young for the class. Better luck next year.

Three years later, it happened again. I flunked the fourth grade. Reading was a problem. I was slow in math. My spelling was (and still is) atrocious. This time I not only flunked the class, but was asked to leave the private school I was attending. Something isn't quite right here, I was beginning to suspect.

At a remedial school, I was placed with fourth, fifth and sixth graders who had similar problems. Somebody determined that my slow reading might be due to weak eye muscles, so I was asked to sit in a room and do eye exercises for an hour at a time. Never mind the fact that my eye doctor indicated that I had 20/20 vision.

I managed to be readmitted to the private school I flunked out of in the sixth grade (joining my original class). My next academic morter attack came in the tenth grade where I, again, flunked the grade. I was attending a very prestigious private school in Connecticut (Choat) and I was, once again, asked not to return. Although I was becoming a scholastic joke, I had started to excel in athletics -- football and track, and if I had not had those successes to buttress me, I think I might have become a very negative personality. At this point, I'd repeated the tenth grade at another school, and finally graduated at the bottom of my class, receiving an overdue high school diploma.

I was awarded a football scholarship to the University of Oregon, only to lose it later, due to academic ineligibility.

By the time I graduated from college, with a meager C-average, I did not see myself as much of a world beater.

I went to work for a local T.V. station as a gopher, only my talents with details weren't very good, and if I was sent to go for ten cups of coffee, I would inverably get the order mixed up. A year later, I lost this job.

In the success column, I had married my eighth grade sweetheart, to whom I am still married twenty-six years later. I had a beautiful son and another child, a daughter, on the way, but I was out of work.

My father had a family business that I had very little interest in (interior design and contract decorating). He convinced me that I should come to work in the family business which was started by my grandfather. I had often heard the expression, "shirtsleeves to shirtsleeves" in three generations... meaning that the flunky, know-nothing grandson would lose the family fortune, if given the chance. This seemed like a better than even money bet to me. So, after working there in a very uninspired fashion for four years, I quit. How, you might ask, could I quit when I was such a proven bottom fish? Where did I hope to go? What could I have been thinking?

The one thing that I enjoyed was an avocation I had picked up. I loved to write stories. I could sit down and entertain myself for hours at a typewriter. I had begun to write every evening -- first for an hour, then two. Finally I was working for four hours every night on short stories, speculation screenplays and T.V. scripts. I had decided, at the age of 25, that I would make my living as a writer... A very cocky idea for a guy who had flunked most his English courses, but I found that I had an imagination for making up characters and story lines, and that I was never satisfied with my work -- always trying to make it better. I was teaching myself to be a better and better writer. Because of my athletics in high school, and because I was always a popular kid with my friends, I had somehow managed to maintain a positive attitude in life. Deep down I suspected that maybe I wasn't very smart, but my ego and upbeat personality tended to say, "Screw it... Who cares?... I won't think about that today."

It turned out that I have a learning disability known as dyslexia. It has nothing to do with I.Q. or intelligence. In fact, some of the greatest thinkers in the world have shared this problem... Einstein, Edison. Einstein was thrown out of his school in Germany, just like me. He had been taught by his uncle to read, but it had been Einstein who, rejected by the school system, had sat alone and pondered the relationship between time and motion. Pretty abstract stuff. Now, Andy... I'm no Einstein... Get me straight on that point, but I found that I, too, could think in the abstract. I could make up things, stories... like Hans Christian Andersen (another dyslexic and school drop-out). Eventually, I began to succeed in this new career.

Once, years later, when I was at Universal Studios, after I had created, written and produced "The Rockford Files," "Baretta," "Baa Baa Black Sheep," among others, I actually read in a magazine that I was a "brilliant" writer... "A true up and coming genius," the article said. Boy, did I have that guy fooled, because I can still remember the disappointment I caused my family. The dire results I predicted for my own future. I had somehow turned from an intellectual ugly duckling into some kind of creative swan and I still don't know how it happened.

Well, that's not exactly true... I know I finally started doing something I really loved. That, more than anything else in my life, except for my wife and family, has served my career.

So you see, nobody should ever give up on him/herself. Support your children... make them believe in themselves, because you never know when the lights are going to go on.

Hang in there...

Best wishes,

Stephen J. Cannell

THE OAK RIDGE BOYS

ENTERTAINERS

...are one of the entertainment industry's most awarded musical groups. They have performed for four United States Presidents and are deeply committed to many charitable causes.

These guys are favorites of mine. I have worked with them off and on for several years and, along with their band and crew, there is not a nicer group of people anywhere. The Oak Ridge Boys are big on practical jokes. I've seen cakes in faces, clothes "misplaced" right before showtime, and other similar episodes. There is also the occasional "big score." One of those occurred last year on Joe Bonsall's birthday.

The Oaks were in Charlotte, North Carolina for a concert in the Charlotte Coliseum. I was to be on stage for twenty-five minutes before they began and, with my help, the decision was made to "get Joe" in front of everyone that night.

While the guys were still in their dressing rooms, I told the audience about Joe's birthday and let them in on the joke. "At one point in the show," I said, "Joe will introduce to you the members of the Oaks. When he introduces Duane Allen--scream, yell, go crazy! For Richard Sterban do the same thing. And for Steve Sanders. But when Joe introduces himself...nothing. Do not make a sound!"

Well, it was hilarious. Every touch went off just as planned. The crowd screamed for Duane, Richard, and Steve, but when Joe said, "...and I'm Joe Bonsall. Thank you very much!," there was silence. He thought his microphone was dead so he said it again. "I'm Joe Bonsall. Thank you very much!" Dead silence. He looked around, saw the other guys laughing, and as 18,000 people sang Happy Birthday, Joe lay down on the stage. He was laughing so hard he couldn't stand up!

Andy Andrews
P. O. Box 2761
Gulf Shores, AL 36547

RE: Your book

Dear Andy:

I can't exactly say that a lot of doors were ever slammed in our faces. However, there were a lot of rough and rugged times in what I call 'the Oaks' gray years,' from late 1974 to early 1977. Those were the true 'make it or break it years' for our little group. I'll explain ...

In the early 1970's, The Oak Ridge Boys were one of the most successful, southern gospel quartets on the circuit. However, the very special qualities that earned us a reasonably decent living were eventually our undoing in the gospel music business. We were known as a bunch of innovative rebels. Our hair was long — our dress was mod — we were the first gospel act to use a full band behind the quartet — and we used somewhat of a 'rock' approach to our concerts. (Actually, that part of our style hasn't changed much! We are still a four-part, gospel-type harmony group, singing country music with a rock approach and a rock band.)

Well, anyway ... there we were, turning off the established gospel promoters who really wanted quartet members dressed alike, down to their shiny shoes, with only a piano for backup and lots of preaching with the singin'. The Oaks, really wanting to take gospel music mainstream, couldn't book any dates with these old-guard promoters who thought we were too country or too rock. And, rock and country promoters wouldn't book us, because — you guessed it — we were too gospel!

Also during this time CBS Records signed us but didn't really know what niche to fit us into. We were slowly starving to death! The CBS bosses had no faith in us. We had little management and booking, except for what we could scrounge up ourselves. And although we had faith in our talents, our heads were hanging a little low.

329 Rockland Road
Hendersonville, TN 37075

Phone 615/824-4924
Fax 615/822-7078

During this time, six people had an impact on our career that helped us believe we were special and that we could make it, if we could just stick it out.

Johnny Cash took us on tour in 1974 and part of 1975, paid us more than we were worth in dollars, and psychologically healed us, by saying we would be a major act someday. We believed it simply because Johnny Cash said so.

Paul Simon, in 1975, flew us to New York, put us up in a big hotel and tapped our harmonies for his big hit *Slip Slidin' Away*. The world didn't know that it was us on the record, but we did. And it kept us going.

Jimmy Dean, in 1975 and 1976, put us on his shows, always inspired us to be our showbiz best and provided some sausage for the table!

Jim Halsey, our manager and "godfather" from 1975 until the present, started booking us some survival dates, inspired us by saying we had the best show of anyone and that all we needed were hit records. Jim always said "you're three minutes away" from being the hottest act in country music history. He made us believe it.

Roy Clark, through Jim Halsey, let us open his shows in 1976 in Las Vegas and beyond. Our tour of the Soviet Union in 1976 with Roy brought us much praise, respect, and most importantly at the time, p-r-e-s-s!

Ron Chancey. Here's where the success begins! Jim Halsey got us released from CBS Records and in 1977 signed us with ABC-Dot Records (later to become MCA Records). Ron Chancey became our producer and found the hit song *Y'all Come Back Saloon*. And the rest is history.

So, yes there were doors slammed on the Boys. (But doors also opened, with time.) There were record company presidents who said we were all wrong and we'd never make it. But eventually there were those who believed. We've been very fortunate; God has blessed us with talent and friendship and a lot of love for singing and each other. Add a lot of gritty hard work and the good fortune to live in America where dreams can come true: The Oak Ridge Boys. A Texan, Duane Allen; a Georgia peach, Steve Sanders; a Jersey boy with a deep voice, Richard Sterban; and a Philly kid, Joe Bonsall, have not only moved mountains, but pushed a few over.

Best wishes to all of your readers,

Joe Bonsall

"Security is mostly a superstition. It does not exist in nature, nor do the children of men as a whole experience it. Avoiding danger is no safer in the long run than outright exposure. Life is either a daring adventure...or nothing."

– Helen Keller

SCOTT ISAACS

STUDENT

...lives in Littleton, Colorado with his parents, Bud and Kaye Isaacs.

When this book was conceived, I wanted a wide variety of people and occupations represented. Their names or accomplishments were to be familiar to the reader. I also wanted a young person.

Finding a young person who had struggled significantly and emerged victorious turned out to be a problem. Child actors had generally not yet experienced a great deal of rejection. And the other young people I found, though some had wonderful stories, had not made a mark of national notice.

Then, I remembered seeing Scott Isaacs on "The Tonight Show Starring Johnny Carson." He had won the National Spelling Bee and not on the first try, either! After contacting his mother, Kaye, and subsequently talking to Scott, he agreed to write a letter for this book.

There is a humorous footnote to this story. When Scott's letter was received, I typed it into our computer for safe keeping. As is my habit, I always spell-check any document for errors with a program designed for just such a purpose. Amazingly, though many thousands of words are available on this program, some words Scott spelled in competition were not there. Neither did my office dictionary contain them.

I had to call Scott to check my work! Read his letter...you'll understand!

SCOTT ISAACS

**2475 East Long Lane
Littleton, CO 80121**

Mr. Andy Andrews
Post Office Box 2761
Gulf Shores, Alabama 36547

Dear Andy,

In the spring of 1989, I became the sixty-sixth winner of the Scripps-Howard National Spelling Bee. It was well known among the other spellers that I had competed in 1988 and 1987 as well. There was an amount of respect for two and three-timers because we knew exactly what to expect. We had been through the competition before.

In 1987, when I was in sixth grade, I became heavily involved in the spelling bee. My teacher immediately singled me out to be a winner, or at least a high placer in the district competition. To my complete surprise, I won, and as a result, moved on to the Colorado/Wyoming Spelling Bee.

I began studying up to 45 minutes a day, from an innocent-looking booklet that actually held over 3000 words to be used in the bee. If I missed a word, my teacher and mother marked my booklet with a hi-liter. To this day, that booklet looks like a Mardi-Gras festival!

From a field of over 250 contestants at the Colorado/Wyoming Spelling Bee, I alone was left at the end. I had won not only this important regional, but a chance to compete in the National Spelling Bee in Washington, D.C.

Washington was great. The staff coordinating that spelling bee treated everyone like royalty and it was impossible not to have a good time! I had studied many more word lists since the regional bee, but the sixth round was my finale for 1987. I got knocked out by "psittacine". It's pronounced like "citizen," but many times more dangerous to spell! I placed 41st out of 185 contestants.

I took another shot at the Nationals in 1988. After studying daily for an hour and a half, yet another booklet became various shades of fluorescent orange and pink and yellow. I was eliminated in the sixth round again--missing "telencephalon". I placed 39th out of 200 spellers. I felt a little more dejected than in 1987 because I had wanted to do better, but two more places just didn't feel...better.

Eight grade came and I was thrust into a totally different atmosphere. I was at a new school and didn't feel like I fit in at all! Since there was no spelling program, I had to organize one. Problems with participants and general apathy from everyone else almost did me in, but I was determined to go back to Washington!

In January, I resolved to learn as much as possible in the next five months. I poured over the dictionary, looking for eccentric words. Spelling became an obsession to me. Almost every night, I would spend three hours studying and memorizing a list of the 104 toughest words I could find. I loved finding out that a tongue-twister such as "niphablepsia" could simply mean "snow blindness".

I breezed through the "district" competition. But the regionals were the exact opposite. As the competition narrowed down to two, we battled for more than a half hour over words like "girandole," "ullage," and "membranate". When it seemed a stalemate was sure, my opponent missed "papyraceous". I corrected it. Then, after much deliberation, I finally won on "writhen". I was on my way back to the Nationals...to try again.

Finally, the great week came. I would spell 218th out of a record 222 contestants. By the second day, I once again felt the intensity of the competition and the toughness of the words. "Tubuliflorous" was my first word, followed by "desuetude" and "trunnion". By that word, only fifteen spellers remained on stage. I cracked my knuckles and went to work on "harridan" and sporran". Only four spellers--the top four in the nation-- were left. I still refused to die, attacking "morion" and "diluvial" as two more contestants were eliminated.

And there we sat, the last two people in the nation to survive the test of torture. We were nervous and tired. He got up first, and nailed "saponaceous". Meanwhile, I almost went berserk trying to figure out "ideaphoria". I finally decided to spell "idea" instead of "ideo" after five unending minutes of uncertainty. I was rewarded by a nod from the judge and the crowd went crazy. I slumped back, thankful for having survived the toughest word in my career. Next, the word was "pasigraphy". Compared to our performance before this word, we were shocked to misspell it--both of us. It was almost anticlimactic.

The next word was "senescing," meaning growing old. He missed it. Surprisingly, I figured out the word while he was up. All I needed to do was ask if the word was related to "consenescence" and "senile". I got up, asked the questions immediately, then nailed it. Everyone cheered. But I knew that one word still separated me from victory.

"Spoliator". As soon as I heard it, I knew the bee was won. I knew exactly what it was--except for the "or". I hesitated for about one minute. Finally, I took a deep breath and looked out at the anxious crowd before me. Then, staring at the judge, I started. "Spoliator...S-p-o-l-i-a-t-o-r...Spoliator." I heard screams and the judge nodded and smiled.

YES!!! I knew I could do it! I pumped my fist, congratulated the second place finisher, and turned back to the crowd, jubilantly exulted. I had conquered the most sought after goal in my short life. I finally reigned, the champion. It was worth everything I had gone through!

Looking back, it seems almost ironic that I actually considered not competing that final year, but I was determined not to give up and was rewarded with my final try. One last note that I think is pretty funny. After I won, I was so ecstatic that I started to cry. But in the midst of all this happiness, my first cohesive thought was, "Oh no! What if my contacts fall out?"

Sincerely yours,

Scott Isaacs

Scott Isaacs

"Man alone, of all the
creatures of earth, can
change his own pattern.
Man alone is architect of
his destiny. The great
revolution in our
generation is the
discovery that human
beings, by changing the
inner attitudes of their
minds can change the
outer aspects of
their lives."

– William James

WARREN MOON

NFL QUARTERBACK

...has now been selected three times as the starting Quarterback in the Pro Bowl. He has a Bachelor of Arts degree in Communications from the University of Washington.

This past season, Warren Moon held the undivided attention of the nation's football fans. As the field general of the Houston Oilers' "run and shoot" offense, he set records as fast as the press could find them in the book. In the process, Warren passed for almost 5,000 yards!

Warren is very active in community affairs. He holds board positions with United Way, The Urban League, and his work with terminally ill children on behalf of Ronald McDonald House is tireless. The Special Olympics also receive a great deal of his time. Children in general, as he proves with his letter, are of particular interest to him.

In 1989, Warren Moon was named "The Travelers NFL Man of the Year." This award, without a doubt, is one of the most prestigious honors that any professional athlete can receive.

Married to his high school sweetheart, Warren considers Houston home for he, his wife, and their four children. Through an exemplary lifestyle, he is a perfect role model for the many young people who watch his every move. Warren Moon is a leader...not only on the football field, but in his church, family, and community.

CRESCENT MOON

F   O   U   N   D   A   T   I   O   N

10777 Westheimer, 5th Floor
Houston, Texas 77042

(713) 956-7100
FAX: (713) 954-8335

Andy Andrews
P. O. Box 2761
Gulf Shores, AL 36547

Dear Andy:

My mother, Pat Moon, knew that lots of free time is not good for kids. My father had died when I was seven and, after his death, she made sure that my four sisters and I kept busy with things like Bible School, Cub Scouts and Sports. There were other kids in our Los Angeles neighborhood who did nothing, but she did not allow me time to hang around with them.

When I was fourteen, I learned the hard way why my mother always kept me so busy. One day, two buddies and I were walking past a drugstore. My friends, who were older than me, wanted to go inside and buy some ice cream. In the store, we saw these neat headbands that cost one dollar each. Since we played on the Sophomore football team at Hamilton High School, the bands would be great to keep sweat out of our eyes. I had about three dollars in my pocket. I could have bought a headband had I wanted to.

But my friends said we could just grab a few, stuff them down the front of our pants, walk outside, and just keep going. I had never done anything like that, but when they stuffed the headbands in their pants... I did too!

As my buddies headed for the exit, a voice on the loudspeaker boomed, "Someone stop those three boys!" My friends dashed outside and got away. I froze. I was searched and a headband was discovered. I was more than scared: I was terrified! I had no idea what they were going to do to me.

The store's security guard handcuffed me and moved me to the side of the store near an exit. Everyone looked at me as they walked past. You know, when it actually happens to you in real life, however, it's a different story all together. Handcuffs are made of steel. They are heavy, and believe me, they hurt.

Meanwhile, the manager had called my mother and told her to come to the store. Facing my mom was the worst part of the whole incident. I knew how much she loved me, and seeing the disappointed look on her face when she arrived really hurt. Right there, I made up my mind never to get in trouble again.

The store manager talked to my mother for a long time. I
think he wanted to scare me... and he did. He did not call
the police, but he wouldn't let me go until I told him the
names of my friends.

No one from the drugstore or police station ever called my
buddies. They weren't bad kids, and I wasn't a bad kid,
either. I just was not thinking clearly when I let them get
me into that mess. I had never planned to steal. I just
walked into a store with friends and "went along with the
crowd."

That was by far the worst day I ever had, but out of it came
a promise to myself to stay away from "the crowd". I wish
every kid could be strong enough to say no in those types of
situations. Sometimes it is tough to do what is right when
everyone around you is doing what's wrong. I know it's hard.
I have been there. And partly because of that experience, I
now run The Crescent Moon Foundation, which holds fundraisers
to help underprivileged kids. It is nice to believe that my
worst experience not only taught me a lesson, but is
instrumental in reaching kids even today!

Sincerely,

Warren Moon

"...we also glory in
tribulations, knowing
that tribulation produces
perseverance; and
perseverance, character;
and character, hope."

– Romans 5:4-5

HUGH DOWNS

BROADCASTER

...is one of the most respected journalists in television today. He is currently the co-host of the highly rated ABC News program, "20/20."

Hugh Downs has been a fixture on television for years. From hosting the "Today Show" to his present position on "20/20," he is one of the most critically acclaimed and awarded television personalities of our generation.

Early last September, I contacted Mr. Downs about this project. The letter I received was amazing...not because of any examples of horrible times or constant rejection; his letter contains nothing even close to that.

Instead, Mr. Downs doubted the value of his letter to this book, because, he says, "I was not singled out [for rejection], but merely was among those who were not chosen." As I read his words, it suddenly occurred to me, that although this man had quite obviously experienced rejection, he simply refused to look at it that way!

How much, then, might we all accomplish with that same mind-set? Everyone has problems. We are all, in one form or another, rejected. The difference for Hugh Downs has been, without a doubt, his attitude.

ABC News 20/20 157 Columbus Avenue New York NY 10023 (212) 580 6014

Hugh Downs

Mr. Andy Andrews
P.O. Box 2761
Gulf Shores, Alabama 36547

Dear Mr. Andrews:

Your book idea is intriguing and I know I will want to get a copy of it, but I'm not sure my experiences would be of use to your theme: I have put what is probably an inordinate time and effort in avoiding situations where I might be rejected and, as a result, have not run into much of what I could call rejection.

The closest I could think of is mass rejection of losing auditions early in my career. In these cases, however, I was not singled out but merely was among those who were not chosen. As a result of this early on I quit auditioning. Every career advance I've had since is a result of somebody asking for me rather than my actively seeking. I do not cite this as a virtue because it probably shows overcaution, but the technique has stood me in good stead both in getting ahead and cushioning myself against disappointment. Two exceptions to this are two pieces of science fiction I published, one in 1964 in Science Digest and the other in 1987 in Omni Magazine. The story in Science Digest was part of a regular column (non-fiction) that I was writing for the magazine -- I merely put that column in fiction form -- and the Omni manuscript was submitted over the phone and accepted.

If any of this is useful to you, you're welcome to it and good luck with the project.

Sincerely,

Hugh Downs

Hugh Downs

HD:jf

ALEXANDER GODUNOV

DANCER/ACTOR

...was born in Russia on the island of Sakhalin. He danced with the famed Bolshoi Ballet for nine years and, in 1979, asked for and was granted political asylum by the United States of America.

Alexander Godunov began his ballet training at age nine. After graduating from the Latvian Dance School in Riga, he joined the Young Classical Ballet in Moscow and, three years later, in 1970, the Bolshoi Ballet. Shortly after joining the Bolshoi, Alexander bypassed the corps de ballet and danced the principal role of Siegfried in *Swan Lake*.

Although he has won numerous international awards, Alexander Godunov is perhaps best known to Americans as the Russian celebrity who gave up everything he had worked for in his life--for the chance to live as a free man. Many people recall the detaining by American authorities of the Soviet airliner at Kennedy Airport that held his wife for 72 hours.

He has now earned critical acclaim as an Amish farmer in the film, "Witness." He struck out in an entirely new direction, playing comedy, in "The Money Pit" and then succeeded in a very convincing portrayal of a ruthless terrorist in the hit movie, "Die Hard."

In the future, when I am tempted to let rejection depress me; I will try to remember Alexander Godunov...a man who risked his very life for the privilege of being able to face rejection.

ALEXANDER B. GODUNOV, INC.

Mr. Andy Andrews
P.O. Box 2761
Gulf Shores, Alabama 36542

Dear Mr. Andrews:

My views about rejection might be different than most peoples in
that my life has taken a different course than most peoples. I
have been fortunate in my careers in the sense that outright
rejection didn't really play a part in my getting an opportunity
to show my art. My success with the Bolshoi Ballet was almost
immediate and I was fortunate that my first acting job was in
the critically acclaimed film, "Witness."

Rejection came into play in the sense that I was not always allowed
to do what I wanted in the Soviet Union. For instance, I was not
allowed to dance outside of the Soviet Union for five years. When
I was finally allowed to tour with the Bolshoi to America, I defected
in New York. My U.S. premiere with American Ballet Theatre was
cancelled due to a dancers' strike. So my first performance was
turned into a television special with the wonderful American ballerina,
Cynthia Gregory.

When my ABT contract was not renewed after several seasons, it was
turned into a public spectacle by the media which could be viewed
as massive rejection on a very public level. I then went on to tour
the U.S. with a small company that I had put together which was very
successful and was taped as a television documentary that has aired
worldwide. Following that tour, I was asked by Peter Weir to appear
in "Witness" because he had seen the documentary and, fortunately, I
had the time to do the film since I was not working with ABT.

What I am trying to explain is that rejection sometimes forces you to
look at new opportunities which can work out for you better in the
long run. If the Soviets had not prevented me from expressing my art
to a worldwide audience, I might never have defected to the U.S.
If ABT had renewed my contract I would not have had the freedom to
explore other avenues of expression such as television and films.
So, as hard as rejection can sometimes be, you never know what the
future holds and it can sometimes be the best thing that happened
to you.

Sincerely,

Alexander Godunov

PHYLLIS DILLER

ENTERTAINER

...has starred in countless major motion pictures. She is a best-selling author and has maintained star status as a comedienne for more than four decades.

Phyllis Diller wrote her letter from a hotel room in Australia. As usual, she was on tour. Phyllis has passed her 70th birthday, but doesn't look or act like it. She manages a schedule that includes performing, writing, television appearances, and interviews.

I first met Phyllis at the airport in Miami. We talked briefly and although I'm sure she wouldn't remember, she was very encouraging to me that day. "There are a million great things about my work," she said, "and only a few things on the minus side. Never focus on the bad--it's a waste of time and energy."

Every time I see Phyllis now, whether I'm talking to her backstage or watching her on TV, the one character trait I consistently notice is her joy. She seems to always be in a wonderful mood. That is obviously a part of her success.

Phyllis Diller

Dear Andy

Shortly after I got my first job as a night club comic
the management changed and I was fired.

I was booked in New York to do a part in a sketch on
the old and much heralded STEVE ALLEN SHOW. After
3 days of rehearsal and much whispering amongst the
bigshots, I was fired and replaced by Jane Dulo.

My great big new important agency who had just signed
me, sent me to the hottest spot in Miami Beach, the
Fontainebleau Hotel. After the first show I was fired.

I went back to New York City where I was living in a
run down cheap hotel ($60.00 a week).

This panicked the big important agency and if it
hadn't been for my precious friend and promoter, Jack
Paar, I don't know how long it would have taken to
eradicate that defeat.

During the first five years of my career as a comic I
was a "Homeless Person" literally. I had no home.
Wherever I had a job that was where my "temporary"
home was.

The way to get ahead in life is just keep pluggin'
away, never give up, don't accept defeat, keep pushing,
onward & upward!

LOVE

Phyllis Diller

RALPH EMERY

TELEVISION/RADIO PERSONALITY

...has been called, "the voice of country music." He is the host of "Nashville Now" on The Nashville Network, the only live, ninety minute talk show in America.

As host of the television show "Nashville Now," Ralph Emery is seen by millions of people five nights a week. As a frequent guest on the program, I see him about once a month!

I often wonder if the man knows how many fans he has. Traveling around the country as I do, I constantly run across people who ask me to relay messages to Ralph as if he is their next-door neighbor. "Say hello to Ralph," or "Tell Ralph I like the red and black tie he had on last week," or a million other things.

It is also funny to me that the same people who have watched Ralph for years, often can't get his name right! "We watch you with Ralph Henry." "Saw you last night on Ralph Emerson." "That Hal Emery is some guy, huh?" I've heard them all. One little girl even came up to me and said, "We watch you on Alf."

But make no mistake, they consider it his show. People may see an entertainer on "The Tonight Show," or the "Today Show," or "Good Morning America," but if a performer appears on "Nashville Now"--they have seen him "on Ralph"!

Ralph Emery

Andy Andrews
P.O. Box 2761
Gulf Shores, AL 36547

Dear Andy,

The year was 1957 and I was the morning man at WMAK, a
rock n' roll radio station in Nashville, Tennessee. A
close friend of mine, Wayne the Brain Hannah, was a
nighttime disc jockey there. For some reason, the
management told me they were going to fire him, but asked
me not to say anything. Well, Wayne's wife was pregnant
and I just couldn't let them blindside him so I told him!
My mistake was that also in the control room at the time
was another disc jockey who was a "brown noser." He told
management that I had let Wayne in on the secret. They
fired me and kept Wayne! What happened next really
rounded out the story. Wayne, not leaving well enough
alone, went into an announcer's meeting, cursed the
program director and got fired anyway!

So there I am...a rock n' roll morning man out of a job.
After several weeks of looking, I heard about an opening
at WSM, the country station. I auditioned for one week,
was accepted, and the rest as they say, is history!

Today, I host a regional television show every morning, am
the spokesperson for several nationally known products,
have a nationally syndicated radio program, and host the
only live ninety minute talk show in the country. With
Nashville Now on the Nashville Network, I am in over 50
million homes, five nights a week.

I have often wondered what my life would be like were I
still a morning man for WMAK. It is certainly true that
somehow our worst times can turn out to be our best. And
it should be encouraging for others to note that in my
case, few of the wonderful things that have happened in my
life would have occurred if the worst hadn't happened. I
was fired!

With ever good wish I remain

Sincerely,

Ralph Emery

RE/ts

KEN STABLER

FORMER NFL QUARTERBACK

...guided the Oakland Raiders to a Super Bowl Championship in 1977. He was voted All-Pro four times and in his career, threw 194 touchdown passes.

I see Ken Stabler every now and then. On the golf course--in the grocery store. He and I live in the same area. In fact, wherever I go in the country, when people find out where I live, they ask about Kenny.

He grew up in Foley, just north of Gulf Shores. He played football for Bear Bryant at the University of Alabama and then on to the Oakland Raiders. Only drafted in the second round, Kenny became one of the highest percentage passers in the history of the NFL.

Kenny Stabler is one of those unique individuals who will always be remembered for his attitude and approach to the game. When Kenny walked onto the field, he was a Top-Gun fighter pilot. Defensive players lived in absolute fear of him because of his reputation. He was a Quarterback who would get the job done, no matter what it took.

He is still considered the "Master of the Two-Minute Drill." No one ever ran it better. Adding to his legend is the fact that during his entire fifteen year career, he never lost a Monday night game!

Kenny is now the Sports Host and Analyst for CNN. He also hosts a celebrity golf tournament every year. To this day, he approaches every project with which he is involved as if the game is on the line. It's a method that has served him well. And whether the object is the end zone or raising money for disabled children, he will get the job done...no matter what it takes.

·T·H·E·
Stabler
COMPANY

Andy Andrews
P.O. Box 2761
Gulf Shores, Alabama   36547

Dear Andy:

When I received your letter and request, one particular subject came to mind.

The majority of people are pessimistic and they put restricting limits on others. These limits become mental barriers, discouraging potential goal breakers from going beyond these preconceived limits.

A good analogy of this is the four minute mile. For many years all of the track and field experts said that no one would ever run a sub four minute mile. On May 6, 1954, in Oxford, England, Roger Bannister ran a 3.594 minute mile. After Bannister broke this mythical four minute mental barrier, the sub four minute mile was achieved by many other professional milers. Today, nearly all of the professional mile runners break a four minute mile.

A similar barrier was placed upon me. As a young athlete, I had visions of being a successful quarterback at whatever level my abilities would take me. Unfortunately, others, such as armchair quarterbacks and second guessers, placing their pessimistic mental restrictions upon me, did not see the same visions as I, simply because I was left-handed. Left-handed quarterbacks were not very common on any level of competition. So why was I to change things? There was Terry Baker from Oregon on the collegiate level and Frankie Albert in the Pros, but not many others.

I used this indirect rejection as a motivating factor to prove to the non-believers and to myself, that I could be an effective left-handed quarterback. I had to prove it at every level at which I competed: at Foley High School, then at the University of Alabama, and once again when starting my NFL career with the Oakland Raiders.

I experienced first hand what telling someone they "can't," will do to motivate one.

Playing a team sport one cannot do it alone. I was very fortunate to have played with a lot of wonderful athletes. But being told I could not do something simply because I was left-handed was a tremendous motivator for me.

Now, thanks to the direction of great coaches, the help of great athletes, and the motivation from being told that I could not do something, I can look back on my football career with feelings of accomplishment and self satisfaction.

I refused to let others decide my limits.

Many people have proven throughout history that great accomplishments seemed at first impossible.

I would like to leave the reader with two thoughts:

1. You can attain any goal in life if you commit yourself to that goal and if you are willing to sacrifice to reach it.

2. Don't let others set your limits; the only one who can stop you is you yourself.

Thank you for the opportunity to express my feelings, and I hope readers will gain from my experiences.

Kindest regards,

Ken Stabler

"...let us run with
endurance the race that is
set before us."

–Hebrews 12:1

AL COPELAND

ENTREPRENEUR

...is Founder and Chairman of the Board of POPEYE'S FAMOUS FRIED CHICKEN & BISCUITS and Chairman of the Board of CHURCH'S CHICKEN. Al Copeland Enterprises, Inc. employs over 30,000 people.

Al Copeland is a native of New Orleans. Having been poor as a child, he grew up planning his "escape from the trap." That escape started from scratch in 1972 with one small restaurant--and a very big dream.

He developed his special recipe to appeal to his hometown's love of highly seasoned food. But the spicy chicken craze he started swept the fast-food industry nationwide, catapulting POPEYE'S into the spotlight. In 1989, Mr. Copeland acquired CHURCH'S CHICKEN, which propelled his company to the number two spot in the fried chicken franchise industry.

His business success has provided Mr. Copeland with the opportunity to combine his personal interests with activities that bring benefit to the community. Virtually every charitable organization in New Orleans has received generous donations. The effort most dear to his heart, however, takes place at Christmas when, with the cooperation of the Archdiocese, Al Copeland provides gifts to thousands of needy children in the area.

Al Copeland's drive has lifted him from obscurity to his position as one of the country's most aggressive corporate leaders. Helping others is just one of the joys that success has brought to a man whose childhood fantasies gave him ambition.

Al Copeland
ENTERPRISES, INC.

Andy Andrews
P.O. Box 2761
Gulf Shores, AL   36547

Dear Andy,

Your request letter stimulated a lot of memories and gave me an opportunity to reflect on some really important events in my life.

My company, Popeyes Famous Fried Chicken & Biscuits, is now 18 years old - about the same age I was when I first started out in business. Looking back, I can see that I probably didn't represent a sure-fire winner to anyone but my family then, and perhaps there were days when they had doubts.

I had a doughnut shop when I began developing my recipe for spicy fried chicken. I used my family and friends as I tested each variation of ingredients. My friends' advice was that while they loved it, the chicken was too spicy for general taste, especially children. When I opened my first fast-service chicken restaurant, "Chicken on the Run", I offered the spicy recipe as a special order.

Seven months later I was awash in red ink and ready to give up. Since customers were willing to wait in order to get the original spicy recipe, I felt I owed it to myself to follow my own instincts and go with it. I changed the name to Popeyes and in just weeks sales reached the break-even point and I had started making plans for three more stores.

In 1989, with 750 Popeyes across the country and in several foreign countries, I purchased Church's Chicken and the merger took Al Copeland Enterprises to the number two and number three positions in fried chicken chains.

When you condense the story as I've done here, it does not convey the long hours, the risks and sleepless nights - or the thrills, the pride of accomplishment or the gratitude I feel for the experience. I started out with limited formal education, which I certainly don't recommend, but I've never allowed that to hold me back. I learned to set goals for myself and my company and to believe in my ability to achieve them.

Sincerely,

Al Copeland

POPEYES CHICKEN FAMOUS FRIED & BISCUITS   Church's CHICKEN

1333 S. Clearview Parkway • Jefferson, LA 70121   (504) 733-4300

BILL DANCE

PROFESSIONAL BASS FISHERMAN

...has won countless professional tournaments. He is now seen every week on his own nationally broadcast television show, "Bill Dance Outdoors."

When I was in high school, I wanted to be Bill Dance. Not be like Bill Dance--I wanted to *be* Bill Dance! As far as I was concerned, he had the best job in the world. I read about him in magazines. I watched him on television. The man fished for a living!!!

As one might guess, I loved to fish. And Bill Dance was my idol. If Bill used Strike King Lures, so did I. If Bill varied his retrieve from one cast to the next, so did I. I tried to do everything just like Bill.

A lot of other kids were the same way. And Bill must have been aware of it. He was a wonderful teacher and a great example. He always ended his television show (and still does) by reminding his viewers to wear their life jackets. He was also one of the first nationally recognized sportsman to publicly advocate releasing the fish to "fight another day." "Keep what you can eat," he'd say, "and release the rest!"

Bill always stressed boating courtesy and a concern for the environment. The impact that he has had on the lives of young outdoorsmen through the years is incalculable. I was, of course, one of those young outdoorsmen and so, for me, receiving a letter from Bill Dance was a special thrill...even if he didn't ask me to go fishing!

Strike King Productions, Inc.

Charles Spence

458 Distribution Parkway
Collierville, TN 38017
901/853-6490

Bill Dance

Televideo Productions

Mr. Andy Andrews
P. O. Box 2761
Gulf Shores, Alabama 36547

Dear Andy:

Thanks for your recent letter. Being on national television each
week, I just naturally receive a lot of correspondence, but yours
is the first that asked me to comment about "failures". To this
end, I believe I could provide you with enough material to supply
an entire volume, and yes -- I agree that many people probably are
under the impression that I have simply "fished my way to glory".
I feel very fortunate to have achieved some measure of success in
my chosen field, but you may rest assured that a lot more has been
involved than merely "wetting a hook" everyday.

From the time I was a very young boy, when I dabbled a hook
alongside my grandfather's in a small creek near Lynchburg,
Tennessee, I dreamed of having a job in the fishing industry. The
advent of professional competitive fishing tournaments in the mid-
sixties provided a vehicle for me to finally realize a part of this
goal. With a lot of hard work and a lot of luck, I managed to win
over a third of the first fifteen events and placed in the top five
of the others. The recognition that went along with these
accomplishments resulted in me being offered my first full-time
position with a nationally-known lure manufacturer. Their plan was
for me to conduct seminars and sales promotions, but moreover they
wanted me to develop and market a television fishing show!

I thought the idea was great, but I had grave reservations about
it. I knew absolutely nothing about photography or post-production
and certainly I had no experience in marketing via the airways.
I dove into the project headfirst, however, because the very
thought of fishing on T.V. and getting paid for it was beyond my
wildest dreams.

For several months, I made daily visits to program directors of
television stations throughout the mid-south area and presented my
ideas for a fishing program. Repeatedly, it was made quite clear
to me that I had a dumb idea. "The couple of fishing shows that
already are airing are barely successful", I was told. "There
aren't enough viewers interested in outdoor sports to establish a
worthwhile following".

Day-in and day-out, similar responses discouraged me tremendously. It became very difficult to stay motivated and I actually started to wonder if the critics were correct.

One night I was discussing my dismay with my wife, Dianne. She reminded that it was much easier for me to convince myself that I couldn't accomplish my goal than to make myself believe that I could do it, and that if I allowed these negative thoughts to dominate my thinking, I might as well quit right now.

That night I went to bed with mixed emotions. Should I throw in the towels and forget about television? Over and over, throughout the night I repeated to myself, "I can. I can. I will. I will. I must!"

By the next morning, my motivation took a new direction, and I set out again with renewed confidence in myself. I would not quit, until I found someone receptive to my ideas.

That very same day a slight glimmer of light appeared in the tunnel when Lance Russell, Program Director for the local ABC-TV affiliate told me, "If you can come up with a sponsor to pay for the air-time and bring me a pilot program that suits us, we'll give it a shot!"

Wow! Finally, I was on my way. But there were yet other unforeseen obstacles to trip me. Potential sponsors were not eagerly awaiting my knock on their door, as I had imagined they would be. "We don't have the budget". "It costs too much!" "Sponsor a what? -- no way!" Are you Crazy?" "A show like that will never go!"

But this time, I knew I would not become discouraged. I had made both myself and wife a promise. I would be on television teaching people what I love best -- fishing! But I had to find just one person willing to take a risk.

Later that year, with tattered ego and seriously slumping finances, I introduced myself to a man named, Bill Woods, sporting goods buyer for a large independent retailer. I presented my ideas and gave my pitch for what was surely the hundreth time in as many days. He listened intently, paused in deep thought for at least thirty seconds, then looked me square in the eye and said, "Bill, that's a helluva good idea. You've got your sponsor!".

I almost fainted!

The rest is fairly well known. Bill Dance Outdoors was born and in the succeeding twenty years our show has progressed from local to regional to national -- even quasi-international broadcasts. Today Bill Dance Outdoors is seen nationwide via "The Nashville Network" and in Canada, Guam, Puerto Rico, Alaska and Hawaii.

This continued success is due to the superb efforts of many talented people, and certainly I am aware that I could have never accomplished it alone. But I also know that it would have never come to pass, if I hadn't eliminated the word "can't" from my vocabulary.

Regards,

Bill Dance

BD/pt

SALLY JESSY RAPHAËL

TELEVISION/RADIO PERSONALITY

...is one of America's most prolific media talents. With her daily television program and her nightly radio show, she logs approximately 18 hours on-air per week; more than any other broadcaster.

I first became aware of Sally Jessy Raphaël several years ago. I was driving late one night and, quite by accident, set the radio dial on Sally. When I reached my destination, I stayed in the car for thirty minutes more listening to her!

On her radio program, she dispenses common-sense advice to people on a wide variety of topics. One person might ask what to pack on a two week trip to Europe. Another will want to know how to deal with an abusive spouse. Sally always has an answer. Even if that answer is, "I'm not sure, but I'll find out for you!" Whenever I listen to Sally, I am impressed not only by her knowledge, but by her wisdom. And she manages, in some way, to encourage every single caller.

Sally's daytime television show is now seen in over 100 markets in the United States, as well as England and Canada. She tapes six shows per week, two each on Monday, Tuesday, and Wednesday. This in addition to the nightly three-hour radio broadcast.

Her husband of over twenty years, Karl Soderland, answered the phone when I was put through to Sally's office one day. I was calling to tell them about this book and ask if Sally would have time to write a letter. Karl laughed when he heard the idea, and immediately said, "Absolutely."

The letter is an inspirational look at some of her beginnings in the world of broadcasting. Even on the printed page, Sally has a way of encouragement that is unique. The attitude she maintains and persistence she personifies are to be admired. In fact, we need more like her!

Sally Jessy Raphaël

SALLY JESSY RAPHAËL

Mr. Andy Andrews
P.O. Box 2761
Gulf Shore, Alabama 36547

Dear Andy:

When I graduated from Columbia University, the Dean of
Announcers for NBC Radio, Pat Kelly, told me that even though I
had the best well-modulated voice for broadcasting, I should go
out and get a job as a secretary or a receptionist -- they
weren't using women. That's when I first became acquainted with
the "R" word: "REJECTION".
    I look back on that time and I have to laugh. It made me
more determined than ever to accomplish in my chosen field.
    Eighteen firings later somehow, like the Peter Principle, I
always got fired "up" -- and was more determined than ever to be
successful. When I came up through the ranks, I came up when
women were <u>not</u> on the air and still did not have a presence on
radio or television. So I was facing even greater competition
-- men! Through all of these firings, I always felt that I was
right -- and they (the bosses) were wrong. I had to -- in order
to be successful; I took that <u>rejection</u> and turned it into
<u>direction.</u> By the way, some of these were justified.
    After spending a lifetime of talking from every perspective,
I've recognized a number of patterns emerging. The more people
I come in contact with, the more information I have on living my
life -- and, the more information I have to turn around and
share with others.
    Have I gotten used to rejection? Absolutely not. It's
taken me a long, long time to learn how to handle the rejection
of my firings -- to balance -- to know that it was all right to
be in the top 10% -- to forgive myself for not being number one,
and to <u>endure</u>. Have I used it to become an accomplished
broadcaster and television talk show host? Yes! Would I do it
again, the same way? You're damn right! That's how I got where
I am today.

Sincerely,

Sally j Raphael

Sally Jessy Raphael

510 WEST 57TH STREET   NEW YORK, NY 10019   TEL 212 582-1722   FAX 212 265-1953

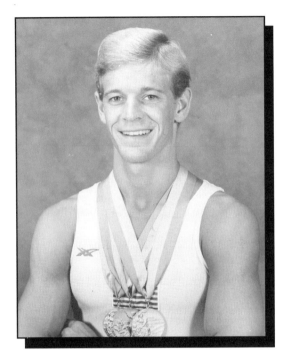

PETER VIDMAR

OLYMPIC GOLD MEDALIST

...in 1984, he captained the United States men's gymnastics team to its first ever Olympic gold medal with a stunning upset victory over the Peoples Republic of China.

The 1984 Los Angeles Olympiad served as a stage for Peter Vidmar to highlight his brilliant career in gymnastics. In addition to his success as captain of the team competition, he excelled in the individual competition. Peter won the silver medal in the individual all-around (missing the gold by just 25/1000th of a point), thereby becoming the only United States gymnast to have ever won an Olympic all-around medal. He then captured the gold medal on the Pommel Horse with a perfect score of "10."

At the Olympic Games, Peter Vidmar had clearly established himself as not only one of the world's great gymnasts, but as an inspirational leader and motivational force as well. He now spends a significant amount of his time translating those skills to Fortune 500 companies. Xerox, General Motors, and Nabisco are among the corporations with whom Peter has worked.

As a television announcer, Peter has covered events for NBC, CBS, and ESPN. He serves on the President's Council on Physical Fitness and Sport and has testified before Congress on behalf of the United States Olympic Committee.

Peter Vidmar now lives in Irvine, California with his wife Donna, a former UCLA gymnast, and their four children.

Vidmar & Company

Andy Andrews
P.O. Box 2761
Gulf Shores, AL 36547

Dear Andy,

It's funny you should ask how my failures affected my gymnastics career. I now believe it was my many mistakes that eventually led to my success in the Olympics. One incident will forever stand out.

At the 1983 World Championships in Budapest, Hungary, I had qualified for the finals on the horizontal bar. Sitting in second place I was a small fraction of a point out of first place. A very difficult skill (that I performed flawlessly in the preliminaries) was my key to a possible Gold medal.

However, in the warm-ups before the finals, I had problems performing that difficult skill and I started to worry (panic). I went so far as to decide to leave that skill out of my routine, to play it safe, and hope for a silver or bronze medal. Realistically, I knew that without that new skill, I couldn't win the gold.

At that point, though, I realized that this may be my only chance to ever become a World Champion, and here I was playing it safe, making it certain that I wouldn't win!

I decided to go for it. The skill involves letting go of the bar, performing a complete flip with a half twist, and catching the bar. Everything went perfetly except the catcthing part. I didn't catch it. Instead, I missed the bar and fell about 10 feet to my stomach.

Needless to say, I didn't even place in the competition. I was devastated. I failed. For weeks I re-lived the fall over and over in my mind.

But from that failure came a deep personal committment to _never_ make that mistake again. Almost every day for the next 6 months before the 1984 Olympics, I would spend extra time on that skill. Fortunately, Horizontal Bar was an event in witch I scored a perfect 10 in the Olympics. Had I never made that big mistake, I'm sure I would not have prepared that skill properly for the Olympics.

I learned an important lesson. It's Okay (even good) to fail.... so long as we learn from our mistakes and improve.

Thanks for reminding me of a terrible but wonderful moment.

Sincerely,

Peter Vidmar

BOB STEARNS

MAGAZINE EDITOR/ WRITER

...is the Boating/ Saltwater Fishing Editor of FIELD & STREAM magazine and the author of several books. His latest publication is A World Guide To Sportfishing.

Bob Stearns is one of those rare writers who brings a reader into a story. When he describes fighting an eight-hundred pound blue marlin, one actually feels the power of the fish and the excitement of the moment. When Bob takes you on a tour of a new boat, you have "seen" it. He doesn't need pictures--his words are enough.

My father gave me a subscription to FIELD & STREAM on my thirteenth birthday. I've read it faithfully ever since. Because boating and saltwater fishing were "my deal," Bob Stearns became "my man." I always turned to his articles first!

Meeting Bob recently was, to me, like meeting a long-time friend. I bored him with "stories of reading his stories," and he indulged me with good humor and, I'm sure, a great deal of patience!

Bob Stearns is good at what he does, but, as is the case with so many things, being good doesn't necessarily guarantee success. In his letter, Bob writes about how he finally achieved success by trying, and trying, and trying. His monthly readers are glad he did!

Field & Stream
Two Park Avenue
New York, NY 10016
(212) 779-5000

Andy Andrews
P.O. Box 2761
Gulf Shores, AL 36547

Dear Andy:

I trust you have had sufficient time to recover from the fine program we recently enjoyed at the 2nd annual Celebrity Waterfowl Hunt in El Campo, Texas. We are truly blessed to both have fun and at the same time help raise very substantial funds for waterfowl conservation. I also laughed until my sides hurt when you did your comedy routine. You are indeed a talented comedian.

You asked about how I got started, and the problems I had along the road to success. So here goes.

When I attended college at Florida State University in the late 1950s, I had absolutely no intentions of becoming any form of journalist. The dislikes I shared with my fellow students about writing "theme" papers in high school were all too fresh in my mind, and my typical outdoorsman's interest in weather, fueled by my father throughout the many hours we enjoyed fishing and hunting together, had already steered me into a curriculum that would lead to a degree in meteorology. Therefore I took no courses in journalism.

After a six year stint in the Navy as a weather officer I settled in Miami and became a Research Associate at the University of Miami School of Marine and Atmospheric Sciences. I spent a total of seven years flying around in hurricane hunter aircraft, but the outdoors always remained foremost in my mind. At the suggestion of a friend, I decided to try my hand at writing for some of the outdoor magazines.

My first attempt was submitted to a small magazine published some years ago by the now defunct Salt Water Flyrodders of America. That publication did not pay for articles, but I figured one has to start somewhere. The letter I got back from the editor was less than encouraging, suggesting that the material was not suitable for publication in the magazine, and also that I might be better served if I pursued some other type of occupation.

Not being able to give it away for free is about as depressing as it gets! But, encouraged by several friends, as well as my lovely wife Shirley, I shrugged off rejections from this and a few other publications, and stuck with it. Then things began to slowly fall into place; eventually I was able to quit my research job and devote full time to doing what I love best.

**Times Mirror
Magazines**

Writing is hard work. Those first few years of "freedom" were lean, and certainly not without some nagging doubts. And even today I still spend many hours at the word processor for each article that appears. A lot of travel time is also involved, which my family endures with amazingly good humor. And great support.

My travels have taken me all over the world, and along the way I have met many wonderful people, especially those who share my enthusiam for the outdoors. Unquestionably that has been my greatest reward.

If I've learned anything from all this, it indubitably is that true success is really never there just for the asking. It requires serious dedication and considerable effort. Plus tenacity. Lots of tenacity, coupled with a desire to succeed more than anything else. And at the same time a willingness to help others, because that too is a vital part of the process.

Andy, I am very flattered to be a contributor to your book. If my comments aid even one person along the pathway toward his or her goals, I'll consider this small effort abundantly rewarded.

Best personal regards,

Bob Stearns
Boating/Saltwater Fishing Editor

"Indeed we count them blessed who endure. You have heard of the perseverance of Job and seen the end intended by the Lord -- that the Lord is compassionate and merciful."

– *James 5:11*

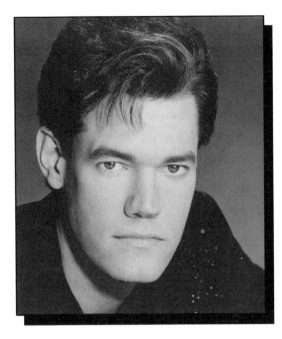

RANDY TRAVIS

ENTERTAINER

...has become a superstar by the age of thirty. His first four albums, all multi-platinum, stayed at "number 1" on the charts a combined 83 weeks.

Everyone knows the story of Randy Travis--how a kid from North Carolina came to Nashville and, along with his manager, almost single-handedly rejuvenated traditional country music. Someone with that story obviously doesn't belong in this book, right? With a voice like his, record companies had to be falling all over themselves to sign him, right? Wait until you read Randy's version of what really happened!

Having known and worked with Randy for several years, I have had the opportunity to spend a great deal of time with him and his manager/mentor, Lib Hatcher. I first met Randy one night in Nashville before I (or anyone else) knew who he was. We talked and laughed a while; then Randy went onstage and sang for about fifty people. Today, less than five years later, Randy is one of the most recognized entertainers in the world. His fans include such diverse names as President George Bush...and Michael Jackson. Of course, I am also a fan. I am a fan of Randy, the person.

Randy Travis is a guy I truly enjoy being around. He's the type of person whom you always wanted for a best friend. He is funny, concerned about other people and their feelings, and he is rarely in anything less than a great mood. His dedication to excellence and his ability to overcome problems, make Randy Travis a person worthy of the success he has achieved...he is also worthy of the admiration that comes with it.

Randy Travis

Mr. Andy Andrews
P.O. Box 2761
Gulf Shores, Alabama 36547

Dear Andy:

I received your letter some time ago and I'm sorry its taken so
long to respond. Unfortunately, we never kept our rejection
letters from the early days because, quite honestly, it wasn't
something I wanted to dwell on.

I did receive my share of rejection though. We spent five years
in Nashville knocking on doors before I got signed to Warner Bros.
Records. We were passed on by all of the labels - several times to
be honest. In fact, the first time I was passed on by Warner Bros.,
Frank Jones who was then the head, told us he loved the voice but
just didn't have a place for me because traditional country music
just wasn't selling.

Jerry Kennedy, who was the head of PolyGram in those days, told
us that he thought women wouldn't know whether to mother me or
take me to bed but, he personally, didn't know what to do with me
as an artist. Dick Whitehouse at Curb Records had a contract on
me for a year but he never took me in the studio and then just let
the contract run out. Noro Wilson, a big time producer, took a
tape from us but then we could never get him to take a phone call
from us to see what he thought.

Then, of course, there's The Nashville Network's "You Can Be A
Star" show which we taped an audition spot for but then never
heard back from them to actually be on the contest. Apparently,
I didn't have what it takes to be a star!

Regardless of who rejected us or how long it took to finally get a
break, Lib and I never gave up the dream. We just knew it was
going to happen - we never dreamed it would be as big as it has
turned out to be - but we never thought of giving up. I think
that's part of the secret - you just have to hang in there if you
believe in yourself and eventually, hopefully, enough other people
will begin believing too.

Best Personal Regards,

Randy Travis
Randy Travis

P.O. BOX 121137, NASHVILLE, TENNESSEE 37212 (615) 383-7258

CAPTAIN WALTER M. SCHIRRA

ASTRONAUT

...was one of the seven original Mercury Astronauts named by NASA in April of 1959. He has logged a total of 295 hours and 14 minutes in space.

Captain Wally Schirra is the only United States Astronaut to have flown Mercury, Gemini, and Apollo missions. That first Mercury flight, which he piloted to six orbits of the Earth, took only 9 hours and 15 minutes. The spacecraft attained a velocity of 17,557 miles per hour and an altitude of 175 miles.

After serving as backup command pilot for the Gemini III Mission, Captain Schirra occupied the command pilot seat on the history-making Gemini VI, which he describes in his letter. Then, he was back in the command pilot seat for Apollo VII, the first manned test of a three-directional spacecraft. That mission completed eight successful tests and provided the first television transmission of onboard crew activities. The five-million mile flight was concluded after eleven days with splashdown occurring in the Atlantic, only 3/10 of a mile from the originally predicted point!

Wally Schirra is still very active in promoting space research. As a man who has "seen the world" from a unique perspective, his views on the work of NASA and what the Space Program means to our future are sought by many. Captain Schirra speaks frequently to corporate and public audiences. It is his continuing effort to maintain the high priority of the research he started over thirty years ago.

Walter M. Schirra
16834 Via de Santa Fe, Box 73
Rancho Santa Fe, CA 92067

Dear Andy,

My first venture into space was on 8 October 1962, and my flight in Sigma 7 was a success. Three years later, after intense preparation, Tom Stafford my co-pilot and I went up the elevator to man Gemini 6 for a launch on 25 October 1965. We went through countdown smoothly and waited for confirmation that the Agena, our target for the world's first rendezvous, was safely in orbit.

No Joy! The Agena failed to attain orbit. No target equalled no mission. Tom and I did the classic fireman's dive, back down the ladder no leap off the launch pad or diving board. Three years of training, simulations engineering reviews and briefings down the drain!

Fortunately, two engineers dreamed up another mission for us. We could launch, from the same launch pad, after Gemini 7 and use them for our rendezvous target. On 12 December 1965,

Tom and I went through another smooth countdown. "Three, two, one ... lift-off" The words came through all the communications circuits, but, in fact I knew that we did not lift off. A milli-second decision by me solved a tough problem. The engines of the Titan booster did start, then shutdown. If we had lifted off a massive explosion would occur on shutdown, We could have ejected to safety. Or we could sit it out, as we did, if liftoff had not occurred.

On 15 December 1965 Tom and I went through a third smooth countdown.

WALLY SCHIRRA

Walter M. Schirra
16834 Via de Santa Fe, Box 73
Rancho Santa Fe, CA 92067

We accomplished the worlds first rendezvous with Gemini 7 on schedule.

Three times, a charm, proved out to us and reinforced the logic about keep trying when the going gets tough. Many rendezvous maunevers have been done since then. Even now, I'm looking at the shuttle crew via satellite television attempting to lock on remote stars beyond where man will ever rendezvous.

Sincerely yours,

Wally Schirra

Mercury 8
Gemini 6
Apollo 7

CHERYL PREWITT SALEM

FORMER MISS AMERICA

...is the author of several books, including her own autobiography. She now tours the country singing and speaking to large groups of people.

Millions of little girls dream of growing up to be Miss America. They enter local and regional pageants. They work on "a talent" and, if they are like my younger sister, even practice the victory walk by strolling slowly across their living rooms. This of course is done with a sheet wrapped around one's shoulders, a cardboard crown, and by waving to imaginary thousands on the couch.

Though many prepare, every year, only one Miss America is chosen. In 1980, it was a young lady from Mississippi. Atlantic City, and indeed the world, watched the crowning of a miracle. Miraculous is the only way to describe the life of Cheryl Prewitt Salem. As you will read in her letter, she struggled against almost overwhelming odds to attain her dream.

Cheryl's work now reaches thousands of people through recorded music, television, and live performances. She also writes best-selling books and teaching materials. Cheryl has found that the best place to coordinate her incredible lifestyle and ministry is in the center of the country--Tulsa, Oklahoma. There she lives with her husband, Harry Salem, II, and their two sons.

C P Annie Productions, Inc.

8252 South Harvard #151 • Tulsa, Oklahoma 74137

Andy Andrews
P.O. Box 2761
Gulf Shores, AL   36547

Dear Andy:

Now that I look over my "preparation" for becoming Miss America, I
believe that one could not imagine a more opposite life style for
success than what I had...all of which could have been used as
"excuses" to keep me in the environment and circumstances that
surrounded me.

My first opportunity not to become Miss America came when I was
born in Choctaw County, Mississippi and lived there in a house on
a dirt road (not gravel, but dirt) eight miles outside of a town
of 2,000 people that did not even have a local beauty pageant to
enter!

My "dress for success" wardrobe consisted of the beautiful dresses
we could make from the flour sacks left in the grocery store.

But you know many people have been poor and overcome their
circumstances to achieve good things in life. Had that been my
only opposition life would have been almost a breeze compared to
what was ahead for me.

It really started with a near fatal car accident I was involved in
when I was 11 years old, which left my face with over 100 stitches
(causing scars that no plastic surgeon would attempt to change);
my back was cracked; my upper left thigh bone was smashed to the
point that when my daddy picked me up out of the car, my leg
literally fell totally limp over his arm as if there was no bone
at all.

That's when I realized life is a series of CHOICES and I was up
against my first big one. I <u>chose</u> to believe during the three
months I was in a wheelchair in an almost complete body cast, that
I <u>would</u> walk again someday -- in spite of what I was told by so
many well-meaning people.

Finally the day came for the cast to be removed. The doctor
declared that a miracle had happened when he saw that a cocoon of
calcium had formed making a bone in my leg that was stronger than
any bone in my body. I could walk!

It didn't matter to me that my left leg was two inches shorter
than the other one so that others called me a cripple and that I
still had scars all over my face and was told I couldn't have

children (due to the injuries I had sustained during the accident). I knew I was a miracle and that the same God who had formed that bone, could also lengthen my leg and take care of everything else...if I wouldn't give up!

After six years of continually making the right choices, and believing God, I was prayed for by an evangelist and my left leg instantly grew two inches.

By now you're probably thinking that these were tremendous obstacles to overcome before walking the runway in Atlantic City in front of over 100 million people. But this isn't even half the story.

Before that wonderful goal was reached, I endured the emotional pain of being sexually abused by a man whom I loved dearly. After several years of this, I chose to believe in myself enough to demand that he stop, no matter if this meant his total rejection of me.

Soon I felt a calling to enter beauty pageants. Shortly thereafter I had another accident in which I fell face-first into gravel, leaving more scars on my face and permanently breaking off my two front teeth. Even after having them bonded back in, I had, and still do, crooked teeth!

So I'm all set to become Miss America -- I am poor, my speech leaves much to be desired, I have scars on my face, crooked teeth, and deep emotional scars! But there is one thing I had that can cause anybody to rise above the circumstances of life -- I had faith in God and in myself. That's all you need. Then based on faith, you can make the right choices. And believe me I had tough choices to make when I began the long road to Miss America, in which I lost for FIVE YEARS.

One thing I learned through all of this is when God puts a dream in your heart it's very important that we take the time to prepare. Without the preparation time, we can get off track, get discouraged and quit. As the saying goes, PRIOR PREPARATION PREVENTS POOR PERFORMANCE. It may have taken me five years, but each year I lost I continued to grow until I was at the place where the Lord needed me to be. I never got discouraged or quit because I knew that God created me to be a winner just as He has each and everyone of us. And when that glorious day was here, I was ready, willing and able to accomplish all that God had called me to do for him when I was crowned Miss America 1980.

Sincerely,

Cheryl Prewitt Salem

Cheryl Prewitt Salem

"Finish every day and be
done with it. You have
done what you could.
Some blunders and
absurdities no doubt
crept in; forget them as
soon as you can.
Tomorrow is a new day;
begin it well and serenely
and with too high a spirit
to be encumbered with
your old nonsense. This
day is all that is good and
fair. It is too dear, with its
hopes and invitations, to
waste a moment on the
yesterdays."

– Emerson

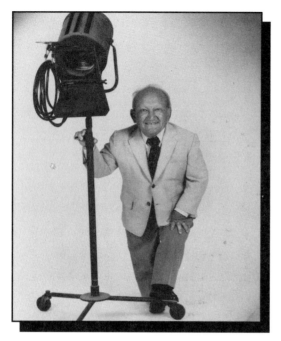

BILLY BARTY

ACTOR

...has appeared in well over one hundred motion pictures. After several decades in show business, he remains in constant demand as an actor and spokesman.

Everyone loves Billy Barty. We've all watched him for years in countless movies, television shows, and commercials. He is the most famous "little person" actor in history. The reviews of his work from fellow performers and industry executives are unanimous in their praise.

But the real respect for Billy comes when one reflects on the courage he most certainly had to muster as a young man. Show business is not a world for the faint of heart, and when Billy was starting out, rejection was a constant companion. He was stared at, sometimes laughed at, and often merely dismissed, but Billy's attitude and genuine love for people lasted longer than his critics.

The work he does for those he considers less fortunate than himself is a daily concern. Billy has succeeded where others might have failed because he keeps his eyes on the future. Bitterness, he knows, is a waste of time, and by sheer strength of character, Billy Barty is a bigger man than most.

BILLY BARTY

Dear Andy,

One question that has been asked of me more than any other question is: "How and why did you go into show business". I started in this business when I was three years old, 17 inches tall, and weighed only 19 pounds. Now I ask you, who do you argue with under those conditions?

As you may or may not know, I am and I have always been a Little Person. If my addition is right, and according to my present age, I have been in the entertainment business for over sixty-three years. Now you want me to relate to the public if I had any rejections. Many, many, many. Most of the times when I auditioned for a part, they all admitted they love my performances yet they rejected me.

Being a little person in this big world is almost an impossible task. My rejections are related to the image portrayed by the movie, advertising and the world itself. One job I'll never be selected for is the Jolly Green Giant. Another is Santa Claus. Yet it states, and always has in the "Night Before Christmas", that Santa Claus is a jolly old elf. I ask you, how can a guy 6' tall and weigh 300 pounds get down a chimney or be pulled by six tiny reindeer, let alone be an elf?

When I got back into the entertainment world, it wasn't easy. The door just didn't open like they would for a Marilyn Monroe or Frank Sinatra. In fact, they never let me play opposite Elizabeth Taylor. I had the talent but being small I was rejected. Jealousy was the major reason for rejection.

Herb Rosenthal was a friend who signed me to an agency contract. He happened to be the Vice-President of M.C.A. In fact, I was on major television in New York for two years and then when I walked into the MCA office in Beverly Hills, they asked me what I had been doing. One of the shows I appeared on was the late James Melton "Ford Festival".

Mr. Melton told me a story many years later about an incident that happened after I had appeared on his show for sometime. Several writers had approached him saying that I should leave the show because they couldn't think of anything more to write about for me. Being the gentlemen that Mr. Melton was, and the respect he had for my talents, he politely told the writers that as long as I was on the show they would be on the show. Needless to say, I was on the show for twelve more months.

How would you like to be rejected for a commercial because they think you can't squeeze the Charmin? I did have an interview to play the side kick for " the Great Gildersleeve" Radio show. It was for Radio so size didn't mean a thing. It was a part for a Little person. I thought I read just great. The director came up and said what a wonderful job I did, but unfortunately, I sounded too tall.

The most important person in life is you. If you can't accept yourself then you have a problem. Be persistent in your endeavors and believe in yourself. Believe in yourself and be prepared to take a thousand no's. Time and one yes can solve many problems.

Sincerely,

Billy Barty

Billy Barty

ROCKY BLEIER

FORMER NFL RUNNING BACK

...was a Vietnam Veteran crippled by enemy rifle and grenade wounds in both legs. He subsequently overcame the injuries and contributed to four Super Bowl victories with the Pittsburgh Steelers.

Super Bowl 1979. The game was tied and the clock was winding down. Bradshaw threw a pass into the end zone--too soon, too high--a pass intended for Rocky Bleier.

Any football fan will tell you the rest; how Rocky leaped into the air, came down with the ball and cemented the victory for the Pittsburgh Steeler's third Super Bowl. And anyone who knows Rocky Bleier will tell you that he's been making spectacular plays all his life.

Rocky was a not-very-big, not-too-fast, but incredibly determined athlete when the Steelers picked him up in the next-to-last round of the 1968 draft. Before he could prove himself as a rookie, he was drafted again. This time, it was for combat duty in Vietnam.

A few months later, after receiving crippling injuries, Rocky faced his biggest challenge. He could barely walk. He certainly couldn't run. To ever play professional football seemed impossible.

In his letter, Rocky Bleier relives a portion of that struggle. His effort to inspire commitment in others continues. He is in demand as a speaker, motivating audiences in a wide variety of organizations, corporations, and universities.

Andy Andrews
P.O. Box 2761
Gulf Shores, Alabama 36547

Dear Andy:

I think most people may think the greatest obstacle that I had to overcome in my career was the wounds I received to both my legs while in Viet Nam. But let me tell you another story that I think may be more important.

The story really begins in 1972. Having spent two years of rehabilitation and working up the Pittsburgh Steeler's ladder from injured reserve to taxi squad I finally made the team. It was a glorious occasion topped off by being the leading rusher during the preseason. The fact that I did not carry the ball once during the regular season did not bother me. I was just glad to have made the squad and play on the specialty teams.

The following year I came to training camp bigger, stronger and faster than I had ever been in my life. I again made the team and again lead all running backs in yards rushed during the preseason schedule. But as fate would have it, relegated to the specialty teams, I never touched the ball again.

In the spring of '74 I started to question my future. Would I ever get a chance to play or be lifer on the specialty teams? Maybe I should get into my life's work, what ever that may be? If I quit now who would blame me. I did make it back when people said I wouldn't. I did play even if it was only on specialty teams. And besides the handwriting was on the wall. Franco Harris and Steve Davis were to be the starting running backs the following year. Preston Pearson and Frenchy Fuqua were to be back-ups. And yours truly back covering kickoffs. Yes I quit!

Shortly after that decision I received a call from our team captain Andy Russell. He invited me to attend a NFL dinner in Chicago. I declined for the above mentioned reasons and told him I just felt that I wouldn't fit in. That, in fact, I quit.

He told me quite sternly that I couldn't quit. That if I quit all I was doing was making it easier for the coaching staff. They, then, didn't have to make a decision. In essence I made the decision for them. He said you can't do that. Don't make it easy for them. Make them make a decision. Back'em into a corner. Don't cut yourself. You make them cut you.

580 SQUAW RUN ROAD EAST   PITTSBURGH, PA 15238   412/963-6763

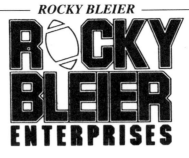

ROCKY BLEIER ENTERPRISES

Well that was the arm twisting I needed. I went back and sure enough my fears came true. Despite leading the team in rushing, once again, during the preseason Franco and Steve started the regular season, Preston and Frenchy were backups and I was covering kickoffs. But in the first game Harris got hurt and Fuqua moved up. By the fourth game I played the entire second half and the next game both Preston and I started. He at halfback, I at fullback. But the end was soon to be in sight. Franco Harris was healthy and ready to play....at fullback. My spurt was over, but at least I played.

The next weeks game was a Monday night game in Pittsburgh against the Atlanta Falcons. In my mind Preston would start with Franco for there was no reason that he shouldn't. You could imagine my surprise when the coach announced that I would start at halfback along side Franco. A combination that lasted seven more years on a team that won four Super Bowls.

I think back on that experience, that if I would have quit you would not have asked me to write this letter to you; I wouldn't have four championship rings and all the memories that go along with it.

Sincerely

Rocky

Rocky Bleier

580 SQUAW RUN ROAD EAST   PITTSBURGH, PA 15238   412/963-6763

"Strive for the approval
of your companions, but
do not be too easily
moved by ridicule. When
you know what you
ought to do, permit not
the laughter of others
to deter you."

– Frederick Starr

JIMMY DEAN

ENTERTAINER/ ENTREPRENEUR

...wrote the six-million seller "Big Bad John." He is currently Chairman of the Board of Jimmy Dean Foods and enjoys time on his 110 foot yacht.

I ran into Jimmy Dean at a Nashville television studio where we were to tape a show. I have always enjoyed the opportunity to talk with him--he is constantly in a state of good humor and has some of the best jokes I've ever heard! As I explained this project and asked if he had a few words he would be willing to share, he smiled and said, "Son, I could write your book for you!"

And so, that's how I ended up reading his letter for the first time only one week later. I laughed as I read it because his words were obviously put on the page with both barrels. Jimmy Dean was waiting for the chance to get something off his chest!

Some years ago, Mr. Dean attended a benefit for a destitute entertainer--a former star. He decided that night that there would never be a benefit for Jimmy Dean. And, believe me, there will not have to be! Even as he maintains his presence in the world of show business, the products of Jimmy Dean Foods have become a favorite of the nation.

As a self-made millionaire, he is convinced that hard work and a belief in oneself are the two major ingredients for success. And I'm not about to argue with him. Jimmy Dean is right!

Jimmy Dean Meat Company
5001 Spring Valley Road/Suite 630E/LB 31/Dallas, Texas 75244-3942/(214) 239-1190/Toll Free (800) 527-9419

Jimmy Dean
Chairman of the Board

Mr. Andy Andrews
P. O. Box 2761
Gulf Shores, AL 36547

Dear Andy:

In your letter you addressed my "success and wealth".
To me, success and wealth have always been a state of
mind. My grandfather, W. J. Taylor, was the most
successful and wealthy man I ever knew, and I doubt
seriously that he ever made more than $10,000 in any
given year in his life. But he was the best farmer in
Hale County, Texas. He knew that. He had the
straightest fences, the cleanest end-rows. He had the
neatest barn and the neatest house. He raised nine
kids; he had a great relationship with the man upstairs
and a wonderful inner peace. To me, this is success
and wealth.

Many look at me and say, "He's the luckiest S.O.B. that
ever lived.". It is true -- I have had much good
fortune, but things were not, and are not always easy.
I have probably had almost as many rejections as
acceptances, but I have ascertained that, were it not
for the rough roads, you would never appreciate the
super highways.

Being knocked down is part of life -- getting up is
also part of life, and people who cannot withstand the
bludgeonings of temporary setback and bounce back, I
have very little use for. Being able to handle
temporary setbacks, (Notice I did not say defeat. The
word defeat is not in my vocabulary.), overcome them,
and stand tall is what entitles you to the sweet bows
of victory.

We, unfortunately, in this wonderful country have
created an element that condones giving up. In my
opinion, when our great President, F.D.R., decided it

was proper that we compensate people for non-productivity, it was the gravest mistake that ever happened.

The good book says, "You'll earn your bread by the sweat of your brow.", as it should be. I have no use for anyone who can help themselves and does not -- reminds me of once when I told my youngest son, Robert, that I was a self-made man, and he said, "That's what I like about you, dad, you take the blame for everything.". It's just that this country has been so wonderful to me, I would like it to remain the land of opportunity for my great, great grandkids.

I feel instead of every day creating another organization for the weak, we should create organizations that make people want to stand on their own two feet and say, "I believe in me.". We cannot create a muddle of mediocrity that makes people feel the world owes them a living.

Every time I talk like this, someone will invariably say, "Easy for you to talk like that; God gave you talent.". Damn right he gave me talent; he gave everyone a talent. My greatest fear is that with all our federal aid, state aid, city aid, county aids, etc. that they're going to be many wonderfully talented people who will never be forced to find out what their talent is.

Sincerely yours,

Jimmy Dean

JD:bmm

"He who never made a
mistake, never made a
discovery."

– Smiles

ART LINKLETTER

TELEVISION PERSONALITY/ AUTHOR

...is the author of twenty books. His daytime show, HOUSE PARTY, ran on CBS from 1945 through 1970.

Art Linkletter was on TV every afternoon when I was a kid. I would have done anything to be on his show. I could just see myself as one of those four children, sitting in a chair at the end of the program, waiting for Mr. Linkletter to ask me a question!

For twenty-five years, his show HOUSE PARTY ran in the afternoons, five days a week. And for twenty-five years, Art Linkletter was able to extract hilarious utterances from the mouths of children. Every single day, some kid would say "the darndest thing." And the nation loved it.

One child might come up with an explanation of how a radio worked or another would tell family secrets. Either way, Art Linkletter entertained a generation by asking the right questions!

Mr. Linkletter now lives in Beverly Hills where he maintains a high profile as a successful author and entertainment executive.

Art Linkletter

8500 Wilshire Boulevard, Suite 815
Beverly Hills, California 90211

Mr. Andy Andrews
Box 2761
Gulf Shores,AL 36547

Dear Mr. Andrews:

In reply to your letter of the 6th:

The most traumatic event in my career occurred in January
of 1939 when I was a 27 year old upwardly mobile performer
and executive in radio striving to become a network program
director. I had taken a job as radio program director for
the San Francisco World's Fair which was to open in February
1939. It was an important job and as a Southern Californian,
raised & married (and career start)in San Diego, I was resented
by some of the fanatically loyal San Francisco group and especially a 70 year old managing director of the whole Fair
who would have preferred a "local" man of his own choice. He
called me into his office a month before the opening date
and after I had been planning the entire schedule of the
official opening asked me to explain my ideas for the grand
opening. I outlined a series of events based upon my experiences at the Texas Centennial of 1936 and the San Diego
World Fair in 1935 (which had thoroughly qualified me for
the job in the first place) which included an appearance by
the president of the U.S., U.S. Marine band, special remotes
(radio only in those days, of course) around the grounds.
He summarily dismissed all this as unimaginative, and when
I asked him if he had any constructive ideas to suggest he
pointed out the window to the Golden Gate bridge and said
"that bridge symbolizes the gateway to the Pacific and the
entrance to San Francisco and if you had any creative imagination and knowledge of engineering you would realize that that
bridge could be used like a giant Aeolian harp!" As I stared
at him in amazement he continued "every steel strand of those
cables holding up the bridge is under a different tension,
like the strings of a harp, and as the wind blows in constantly from Hawaii to the bridge, each steel strand would have a
different hum as the wind speeds by. By connecting a series
of 100 microphones to sections of the bridge and attaching
them to a giant control board, a team of trained sound engineers could manipulate the microphone controls like a
keyboard and use the entire bridge to play "California Here
I Come!" I looked at him in utter disbelief and blurted out
"you sound like a nut." And he said "and you, Mr. Linkletter,
are fired."

That was to be the key event in my life because I went home
to think about what had happened to me and I realized that
as long as you are working for an organization and you have
a boss in the creative business, you can be fired.

I told my wife that I would never again have a boss or work for an organization but rather I would free lance and have a variety of sponsors on shows I would write, produce, sell, and perform in ---I would also take all the money.

Within 3 months I was making twice the salary the Fair had offered, with shows utilizing my knowledge of world fairs and I went on to become a most successful broadcaster in the Bay area for the next five years, making, in the early '40's $100,000 a year, which would be comparable to a million in today's inflated dollars, and eventually Hollywood beckoned and I left to try for even newer horizons with a new show idea I had called PEOPLE ARE FUNNY. My new partner in Los Angeles was a brilliant man who had a similar idea and we pooled our talents to produce the first of the stunt shows on the air and was to last 19 years on NBC, going into television in 1950. We also originated HOUSE PARTY which was on CBS five days a week for 26 years.

The lesson we learn from this is to make the best of what happens and do what you like to do best, and finally, of course, work hard and persevere.

It was the most exciting time of my life when we were inventing a new medium of audience participation shows and writing history in this great medium.

Cordially,

AL:lr

"There is no gathering the
rose without being
pricked by the thorns."

–Pilpay

JOHN AMATT

**MOUNTAIN
CLIMBER**

...was a member of the first successful British expedition to climb Mt. Everest. A motivational speaker, he travels the world, addressing corporate and professional groups.

A friend in Washington, D.C. called me one day with great news. She had just heard a man speak who, she was positive, would be perfect for this book. His name was John Amatt. "He has an astonishing story," she told me, "and you absolutely *must* call him!"

I'm glad that I did!

In addition to the conquering of Mt. Everest, John was the first person, at the age of twenty, to climb Europe's highest and steepest precipice--the 5,000 foot "Vertical Mile" Troll Wall in Norway. In doing so, he spent ten days gradually ascending on minute ledges.

He has also led an expedition to Western China, which made a bold ski ascent of 24,757 foot Mt. Muztagata--the highest mountain in the world to be ascended and descended completely on skis!

John Amatt is now an internationally-renowned speaker and President of the ONE STEP BEYOND Adventure Group, an organization which coordinates adventure-related promotions and wilderness-based management seminars for major corporations throughout North America. He genuinely enjoys his work, for John Amatt has found that in life, as in mountain climbing, the most important part of the climb...is the journey.

One Step Beyond
Adventure Group

Suite 203, 749 Railway Avenue
P.O. Box 990, Canmore, Alberta
Canada T0L 0M0
In Canada: (403) 678-5255
In United States: 1-800-661-9400
Fax: (403) 678-4534

Mr. Andy Andrews
P.O. Box 2761
Golf Shores, AL
U.S.A.   36547

Dear Andy:

I am constantly amazed at how small, seemingly unrelated events – when added together over a period of time – can have a major impact upon the outcome of one's life.

When I was a kid, I tended to view my life as somewhat of a failure. I was intensely shy – so shy in fact that on one occasion I refused to get out of our family car when my father told me to ask directions from a stranger in an unfamiliar town. The thought of speaking to someone that I didn't know left me shaking in my boots. Later in High School, I recall having to repeat a grade because my marks were not good enough. At the time, I was ashamed of this "failure", but when I look back today it seems like the best thing that could have happened to me. Why? Because it taught me the value of "struggle" – that we only really appreciate things in our life that we have had to fight to achieve.

The problem was, of course, that I was not cut out for academic success. This was not one of my strengths! Although I later completed my degree in education (much to my surprise!), I discovered in school that there is no such thing as failure if we come out of a negative experience with more knowledge than when we went in.

My first experience of true personal success came when I discovered the sport of mountain climbing. Here was something that I was good at – something in which I could excel. I started to gain the respect of my climbing friends and to develop the self-confidence that had been lacking in my earlier life. Although I am to this day a basically-shy person, I now make my living giving motivational talks to major American corporations. In fact, I once spoke to an audience of 6,000 people from the stage of Radio City Music Hall in New York. And I told them the story of how I had once been afraid to leave the car and speak to a stranger when I was young.

One Step ▲ Beyond
Adventure Group

Aldous Huxley once wrote that ... "Experience is not what happens to you. Experience is what you do with what happens to you". This has become one of my basic beliefs. I'm constantly seeking out new challenges - new experiences - and learning new lessons. I'm becoming better everyday because of my belief in "positive dissatisfaction for the way it is". I'm always dissatisfied with my performance, constantly trying to improve it in a positive way.

At the age of 20, with two companions I was part of a climbing team that made the first ascent of the world's highest vertical rock wall - the 5,000 foot sheer "Wall of the Giants" in Norway. Before we went to Norway, people told us we were crazy! They told of stories of rocks dropped from the summit that hit nothing until they landed on the valley floor a vertical mile below. The world's best mountaineers said that the climb was impossible. But we proved them all wrong by our willingness to try, to get started on the ascent. Sure we were scared, but we knew that we could not achieve eventual success unless we got started. Having committed to the attempt, our pride helped to overcome our fear of failure. By taking it one foot at a time, we finally reached the summit ten days later. Afterwards I recall saying to myself ... "If you can do that, you can do anything!"

It was around this period that I set my sights on climbing Mount Everest, at 29,028 feet the highest mountain on earth. But it was to be 16 years later before that dream was fulfilled. Along the way, there were setbacks, but each time I ran up against difficulty I learned something new. So it was all of these experiences, which seemed like failures at the time, that eventually took me to the top of the world.

Life is a great adventure. There is so much opportunity for people who are willing to go out and challenge themselves. We all have our own "Everests" to climb - and we can all reach the top if we take it one foot at a time.

Good luck with your own ascents and "Keep Climbing".

Sincerely,

John Amatt

"The glory is not in never
failing, but in rising
every time you fail."

– Chinese proverb

MELVIN BELLI

ATTORNEY

...is the senior partner in the law offices of Belli, Belli, Brown, Monzione, Fabbro & Zakaria. He maintains offices in seven California cities and Washington, D.C.

Melvin Belli, despite a career spanning more than a half-century, remains involved in newsmaking and lawmaking cases. He is still interested and most proud of his work "defending the rights of the individual in a system stacked against the little man."

Some of Mr. Belli's clients have included Mae West, Errol Flynn, Tony Curtis, The Rolling Stones, and Lana Turner. He has also represented many clients involved in mass tragedies over the years such as the MGM Grand Hotel fire in Las Vegas and the Alaskan oil spill. Melvin Belli is perhaps best known, however, for his defense of Jack Ruby, the man who shot President Kennedy's assassin.

His life and legal career were the subject of a recent CBS-TV movie. He has been featured on the cover of LIFE magazine and though his schedule allows him little spare time, Mr. Belli has authored 62 books.

Melvin Belli loves his work, and today, he's just as driven as ever. At the age of 83, he is still in his office every day!

Mr. Andy Andrews
Post Office Box 2761
Gulf Shores, Alabama 36547

Dear Andy,

Back in the summer of 1933, I graduated from Boalt Hall School of Law, University of California. This was during the Depression and jobs for lawyers and everyone else were nonexistent.

I accepted a position with one of the "Alphabetical Agencies" requiring me to write a report on what "bums" really thought about and wanted.

Having no funds with which to travel and gather my research, I slept under railroad tressels, at Salvation Army Halls, in open fields, and indeed in many jails. Particularly one in San Diego, California. I was brought before the villainous Judge early one morning and calling me by my assumed name, he boomed, "Luis Bachigalupi, what do you plead to the charge of vagrancy?!" I said not guilty and told him I wanted a jury trial. After making a comment about "having a smart one here," the Judge instructed the clerk to give me a trial date...for the next year!

Back in my cell, I was quickly convinced by the "good guy" bailiff to change my plea to guilty. The Judge then said, "You Bum, get out of here. I'm going to give you a one year suspended sentence, but if you ever come back here you'll serve the whole sentence."

To make a long story short, I did come back. Two years later, I tried my first jury trial in San Diego and won my client $100,000. for a leg amputation, a record amount at that time.

Incidentally, transients in those days arrived in the Southern California area by the thousands, wanting nothing more than work. The law stated then that if they did not work, they were guilty of a crime called vagrancy. My record of "Guilty to Vagrancy" and one year suspended sentence along with my finger prints of "Luis Bachigalupi" are still on the records in the San Diego Court. The report that I wrote after the incident was used as the basis of "Transient Relief" by the Federal Court and fortunately, vagrancy was declared unconstitutional.

Keep pushing. Work hard and work smart, and maybe, together, we can change the world!

Best Wishes,

Melvin M. Belli

MMB:amp

"Like the shadow of a tree, our influence often falls where we are not."

– *Anonymous*

ANGELO DUNDEE

BOXING TRAINER

...has played a major role in the development of twelve World Champions including Muhammad Ali and Sugar Ray Leonard.

Since December of 1960, the Angelo Dundee name has been forever intertwined with that of Muhammad Ali. After a 21 year ring partnership which impacted the far reaches of the world, both names are indelibly linked. But even the most avid fans are sometimes affected by a short memory. Ali was not the only feather in Mr. Dundee's cap. He developed eleven other World Champions including Sugar Ray Leonard, Michael Nunn, and Pinklon Thomas.

Mr. Dundee told me over the phone that the motivation for writing his letter comes from a desire to "inspire kids." Angelo Dundee has been helping young people for years. At the Miami Beach Fifth Street Gym, young boys who walked in carrying their gear in paper bags, ill-fed, and weary, never left hungry if Mr. Dundee was there.

He has been named "Boxing's Manager of the Year" and has been inducted into the "World Boxing Hall of Fame," but Angelo Dundee is approaching the next quarter-century as if his career was still in infancy. "Enthusiasm," he says, "is the key. And my enthusiasm for the future is running higher than ever!"

PHONE: (305) 625-9999
FAX: (305) 620-4584
CABLE: CHAMPBOX

1505 N.W. 167th ST.
SUITE 405
MIAMI, FLORIDA 33169

Andy Andrews
P.O. Box 2761
Gulf Shores, Alabama 36542

Dear Andy:

After reading your letter, I got to thinking about how I got started in boxing and I can assure you that any successes I have enjoyed didn't come easy.

After seeing a bit of Germany, France and England while with the Air Force during the big war, I looked forward to a calm and normal life back home in Philadelphia. Once back home, I picked up where I left off, as an aircraft Inspector with the Philadelphia Navy Yard. I was comfortable on the job with all the great fringe benefits and security but despite the recognition I was gaining on the job, the boxing game was tugging at my soul. You see, my brother, Joe Dundee, a tough prelim boxer around Philly, laid a foundation of interest for the rest of the family.

My brother Jimmy and I both loved boxing. I had done some neighborhood recreational center boxing, and later, while in the military. My older brother, Chris was one of the hustlingest fight managers in New York and was developing a major reputation. We were hearing about it all the way to Philly and deep down, I wanted to follow in his footsteps. My conflict got a shot in the arm when Chris called me in Philly and suggested I come to New York and break-in to the boxing business.

With some trepidation, I took a sabbatical from my cushy 9-5 job and off I was to the Big Apple, world headquarters for boxing. It would be some time to come whether the conflict, in my own mind, would prove I was doing the right thing. When Chris said "break-in" I didn't know he meant sleeping on his office couch, dreaming about three squares a day and putting in limitless hours each day. 1948 was a tough year in post-war New York boxing and everybody was struggling. Boxing was at the beginning of a revolution, going from all the small clubs and being piped into living rooms via television. Competition was fierce and I was in a learning phase so I worked all the harder. Chris was showing me the way and he was a master of the sport. I started from the bottom, doing the lowliest of jobs, trying to soak up every facet of the game. I kept my eyes and ears open and worked with the venerables like Ray Arcel and Charley Goldman. I watched the Professor himself, Jack Kearns, and I learned plenty about training fighters from my buddy, Chickie Ferrara.

PHONE: (305) 625-9999
FAX: (305) 620-4584
CABLE: CHAMPBOX

1505 N.W. 167th ST.
SUITE 405
MIAMI, FLORIDA 33169

My goal was to teach boxing and train boxers to give their best performance. I was satisfied with my progress but it was touch and go if I could continue with the financial strain. While apprenticing, the money was hard to come by and thoughts of returning to my old job persisted. But I persevered and soon I was joining brother Chris in Miami Beach where he was now operating a new boxing club. New vistas were opening up for me but hard work and long hours were the order of the day. Meager income still plagued me because I was starting a family of my own. However, I stuck doggedly to my work until my first breaks arrived.

After a couple of years at Miami Beach, my financial position stabilized but a new challenge arose. As I gained in experience, the call on my time compounded. I found myself in travel status much too often. I had a family to consider but my work called for more air time than on the ground. My career was taking off and I had to move with the boxers in my care. My travels with boxers found me in the remotest corners of the world and sensitive moments arose which took years to adjust to. Happily, my growing family learned to cope with my erratic schedule and all's well that ends well.

I have always treated the boxers I handle with the deepest respect and with their welfare in mind. In this way I find I get them to perform at their best. When I'm out of rhythm with a boxer's personality, I adjust and tune in with his. I'm flexible. You have to be in order to resolve the complex needs of a professional boxer. I have applied the same attitude toward life in general. When problems of any sort or nature arise, they are meant to be licked. There is always more than one way to skin a cat and intelligent people always find a way to overcome barriers to their lifestyle and make life work.

Sincerely,

Angelo Dundee
AD/blm

132

"God is the silent partner
in all great enterprises."

– *Abraham Lincoln*

MEL TILLIS

ENTERTAINER

...is successful as an actor, author, and musician. He has also been named Entertainer of the Year by the Country Music Association.

Mel Tillis is one of the funniest people I've ever met. Every time I see Mel, he makes me laugh. Out loud. He is also a nice guy. He spends an extraordinary amount of time after every concert signing autographs, having his picture made with children, and "just visiting."

Mel recently acquired his own theater in Branson, Missouri, where he performs for several months a year. It gives him a chance to be with his family more often and still do the shows he loves so much.

He is one of a very few entertainers to appeal to so many different types of people. The movies he's done with Burt Reynolds, Roy Clark, and others have enhanced the "all around" aspects of his career. His autobiography, *Stutterin' Boy*, appeared on several best-seller lists and, of course, he has been making hit records for years.

People identify with Mel Tillis. Not because he has a stuttering problem, but because he has *overcome* a stuttering problem. Understand, he still stutters...it's just not a problem! Mel has an amazing attitude. He took an impediment--and turned it into a logo. Painted onto the back of his tour bus is "M M M Mel."

OZARK THEATER

Dear Andy:

I hope the following story is what you are looking for.

I remembered in 1938 a puppet show coming to Woodrow Wilson elementary in Plant City, Florida. Well that was it! You could say it was my first brush with show business. Today kids can escape into the make-believe of the television set, but nobody had television then. I made my own little theater out of a cardboard box. My performers were made of paper. For actors, I cut out pictures of men and women from the Sears and Roebuck Catalog. I even cut out pictures of furniture for my play-like productions.

I was alone alot, so I did little plays on my make-believe stage downstairs beneath that garage apartment. Most of the time I was the whole audience, except one time when Mrs. Smith, an elderly lady who lived next door, came to one of my productions. She said she was very impressed and gave me and my paper actors a standing ovation.

My pretend theater, the Sears and Roebuck catalog, and the singing at school helped me through that first year at Woodrow Wilson elementary. I was feeling pretty good until the last day. That's when I learned that the teacher who liked my singing so much was failing me.

The other kids were moving up to the second grade, and I wanted so much to be like them and with them. We were getting to be real friends. But I had to stay back in the first grade. I remember I cried and cried. It wasn't my letters or numbers, I'd made all S's. It wasn't for bad behavior either. Miss Clark told Mama she was separating me from my friends because of the stutter and felt that if I repeated the first grade, I might learn to speak "right". I didn't.

Since my childhood productions of little plays in that garage I'd always been fascinated by theatrical things. Many year later, when they were doing the junior play at Pahokee High School. I made up my mind to be a part of it. Nothing was going to stop me, even the stutter that held me back years earlier at Woodrow Wilson. I went to the teacher who was producing and directing the play, and told her that I wanted a part in "Here Comes Charlie". She was surprised and somewhat uneasy. She didn't want to hurt my feelings. She tried to be tactful. "I'm sure you would be good, Melvin," she said, "but...uh...you see...the speaking parts might...well be difficult for you."

HCR 1 Box 721-10 • Branson, Missouri 65616 • Telephone: (417) 335-MMEL(6635)

I thought about that for a few seconds. I was disappointed, yes, but I could understand. Still, I wasn't about to quit. "Then...then...let me puh...puh...pull the curtain," I answered. "I'll be the best curtain puller you ever had."

She smiled and then she nodded. She could understand,too.

So I was part of the play. I'd won. That stuttering didn't keep me out - no sir. I was with Richard, my brother who happened to win the role of Charlie, and the others for all the rehearsals, and when people applauded at the end of the show, I felt I'd earned my piece of that. The teacher even introduced me.

Sometimes I remember that experience when I'm on stage of working in a movie or television production. Beginnings are something that stars, executives, and others shouldn't lose track of, no matter how important they become. The curtain pullers of the world count, too. There's no show without them. They're doing their share, and they're entitled to respect like everyone else.

All the best,

"A task without a vision
is drudgery; a vision
without a task is a dream;
a dream with a vision is
victory."

– *Anonymous*

FLORENCE HENDERSON

ACTRESS

...is best known for her work on the long running television series, "The Brady Bunch." She is now a spokesperson for WESSON OIL and has her own program, "Country Cookin," on The Nashville Network.

My sister lived for "The Brady Bunch." It was the one show that she never missed...ever, even when it started running on local stations every afternoon. My sister is married and living in Florida now, but she still got excited when I told her about getting a letter from Florence Henderson.

I was excited, too. Florence is a lovely lady who is always quick with a smile or a pat on the back. Her show business beginnings have made her especially compassionate to young people who are just starting their careers. Her longevity as a public figure has been due, in no small part, to her genuinely wonderful attitude.

She presently lives in the Marina del Rey section of Los Angeles. A hectic schedule, however, rarely allows time at home. Florence is perpetually in motion as an actress, singer, and spokesperson. Those activities, coupled with a weekly show on The Nashville Network and appearances for charity functions, make Florence one of the busiest ladies I know. And I'll bet she won't ever slow down--she enjoys it too much.

Florence Henderson

Andy Andrews
P. O. Box 2761
Gulf Shores, AL 36547

Dear Andy,

I suppose being born the youngest of ten children to a very poor farmer and his wife in a tiny little river town in southern Indiana could be a perfect setup for rejection. Outside of being made fun of a few times, for the clothes I had to wear (or the lack of clothes I had to wear), or for the awful shoes, I never really let it bother me too much. The fact that I could sing and was accepted for that at a very young age certainly helped ease the sting of those rejections.

The first "professional" rejection I remember was from Horace Heidt, who was very famous when I was a kid. He had his band and a big talent show and travelled all over the country choosing talent for his radio program. Dick Contino was his big star at the time, having won for weeks in a row.

I was going to high school in Owensboro, Kentucky and I heard that Horace Heidt was coming and that auditions were being held at the local radio station, WOMI. Everyone encouraged me to go down and try out. I didn't know you were supposed to have a piano player accompany you. (I didn't have one, anyway!) I was crazy about Jane Powell and saw every movie she made and knew all of her songs, so I took along one of her recordings. Of course, the songs weren't in my key, but that didn't stop me. On one side was "It's a Most Unusual Day" and on the other was "Les Filles de Cadiz," a French song. Of course, I had a very thick Kentucky accent. At the audition, they played the record and I sang along with Jane Powell. Well, I wasn't chosen. They picked another girl and I remember going to the sports center in Owensboro to see Horace Heidt that night and to hear the girl who had won. I was happy for her, but my sister Marty sent a note backstage saying that Horace Heidt had made a terrible mistake and that I was going to be a big star and that he'd probably never hear from the other girl again. That was my first rejection and I felt pretty bad about it. (Marty was right; I can't even remember that girl's name!)

My spirits were undaunted. Shortly after being turned down by Mr. Heidt, I was lucky enough to find sponsorship to study at the American Academy of Dramatic Arts in New York. The family of a friend was wealthy and they believed enough in me to help me realize my dream. While a student, I went to an open audition and was cast in a show called "Wish You Were Here," directed by Josh Logan. For some reason, they let the leading lady go. I auditioned for that role and for any female role that became vacant. I didn't get any of those parts, either, but I didn't get discouraged because I was working in a real Broadway show, being directed by the great Mr. Logan.

Shortly after the show opened, I heard that anyone could audition for Rodgers and Hammerstein by sending in a card requesting an appointment. After I sang and read a scene for them, they called me back again. Both Richard Rodgers and Oscar Hammerstein were there at the St. James Theatre. I sang and read and they gave me the role of Laurey in "Oklahoma" and toured all over the country for a year. That led me to "The Great Waltz" with the Los Angeles Civic Light Opera and while in Los Angeles I screen-tested for "my" role of Laurey in the movie version of "Oklahoma."

Shirley Jones got the part and while I loved her work, that loss really upset me. In order to get the screentest, I had agreed to do another season of "Oklahoma" and while I rehearsed in New York, I was still feeling hurt. I guess I cried a little, but I didn't feel like giving up. I went back on the road for another year of "Oklahoma" and probably learned more that year than in any other.

It's strange how just when you think nothing good can come of a situation, that's when something wonderful happens. Josh Logan called me to audition for "Fanny." After several auditions, commuting back and forth between Boston and New York, it was clear they were having a hard time making up their minds. The tour ended and I went back to visit my folks in Indiana and Kentucky. I had no sooner got home that I got a telegram saying I'd gotten the part and to return to New York. I did "Fanny" on Broadway with Ezio Pinza and Walter Slezak and I felt it was a great reward, in place of the movie role. It was a wonderful time in my life because it enabled me to be in New York for a long period and to study and learn my craft and develop technique, and I'm very grateful for that.

Another rejection was trying to get on the Jack Paar Show. I'd tell my agent, "I really think I'd be so good with Jack," but the agent kept saying "No. He likes Genevieve; she's French, she's offbeat..." but I believed we'd be a good combination. It was so tough. Finally, I got on the show through a fluke. I was singing with Bill Hayes, a very fine performer, and we were rehearsing for a performance. Someone fell out of the lineup for Jack Paar at the last minute and they called us. We went on and I did something funny that Jack liked and, of course, I became a regular. I had persevered. When my agent told me how wrong I was, my gut instinct told me the opposite and I stuck to my guns.

I don't think I've ever felt like quitting. There have been lots of roles I've wanted and haven't gotten, but I've gotten so <u>much</u>. Often an experience is disappointing at first, but you discover that <u>it's</u> set you on a road that brings even greater rewards. If I'm rejected for something I always think that I'm being saved for something better! In other words, I always believe that everything works itself out to the positive.

Most Sincerely,

Florence Henderson

"The greater the obstacle
the more glory in
overcoming it."

– *Moliere*

SI FRUMKIN

WRITER/SPEAKER

...is a survivor of the Holocaust during World War II. Today, he continues his efforts to obtain the release of Jews still in the Soviet Union.

When I read Si Frumkin's letter, I reflected for a moment on a few of the problems in my own life which I had previously considered "major." Believe me, I have a new perspective.

Si Frumkin, at the age of ten, became "Number 82191" of Dachau, one of the most brutal concentration camps in Nazi-held territory. Over 40,000 of his fellow townspeople were herded into this ghetto of barbed wire and gun towers. After four years, only 7,000 survived to be deported. The women were sent to Poland; the men to Germany. Si's father died "of weakness" only twenty days before Dachau was liberated in 1945.

Today, Si Frumkin lives with his wife, Kathy, in Studio City, California. Family photos hang in the entry of his house, and history has given them a haunting effect. That Si Frumkin is even alive bears evidence to a certain success. But the fact of his accomplishments despite incredible odds...is nothing short of miraculous.

Si Frumkin
3755 Goodland Avenue, Studio City, California 91604
(818) 984-1424
FAX (818) 766-4321

Dear Andy:

I was sentenced to death for the crime of having been born. I was lucky. I cheated the executioner. My father, my grandparents, my uncles and aunts, my cousins, my friends - all died. They were all criminals, guilty of the same crime as I was: being alive!

This happened a half a century ago, in a faraway place, to people who spoke a different language than we do, people with whom we have little in common except for a desire to live and the ability to feel pain. It happened at a time when an evil philosophy divided humanity into humans and subhumans, those who deserved to rule and prosper, and those whose very existence was an abomination and who had to be rooted out. It was a philosophy that glorified violence and strength and war, and it succeeded in conquering most of Europe and ridding it of 6 million of my kind.

My kind? I am a Jew.

Let me digress for a moment for I can see your eyes glazing over - yeah, yeah, sure, the Holocaust and the nazis and the Jews and all that, and didn't we hear all about it already, and hey, what's the relevance to today? I believe that there is a relevance, for human nature hasn't changed all that much in the last 2000 years, and surely not in the last 50.

Have you thought, for example, what our world would have been like if Hitler had won the war? Obviously, I wouldn't be here writing this letter; I and all the other Jews in the world would be dead. We would not have been the only ones murdered - blacks, Indians, Gypsies were also subhuman and they too would be dead. Africa would have been emptied of blacks by atomic or chemical weapons, Latinos with more than 1/4 Indian blood would join the Gypsies in efficient death factories, and the history books would tell us of that great and wise man, Adolph Hitler, who half a century ago cleansed the planet of the evil, corrupt, disgusting subhuman races.

But enough of this; you said that you wanted to know about my life, so here goes. For the first ten years of my life I didn't know that a powerful dictator of a great country had sentenced me and my family to death, that it was only a matter of time before the sentences might be carried out. I grew up in Lithuania - a free and independent country at the time - and my early memories are of school, homework, friends, vacations that were much too short and teachers who were much too demanding. I was 9 when the Soviet Union occupied Lithuania and 10 when the Germans attacked the Soviet Union and captured Kaunas, the city we lived in, in just 3 days. Later I found out how lucky we were to have been living in a large city - special units that followed the advancing armies rounded up and killed all Jews that lived in the countryside and the smaller towns. Jews were allowed to live only in the 3 larger cities - they were put behind barbed wire and used as laborers.

I was lucky. I managed to hide when they came into the ghetto searching for children and old people, those who couldn't work and had to be killed at once. I was lucky when selections were made and people were taken away to be shot at an old Russian fortress 10 miles down the road. The first dead body I saw was that of my grandfather - that day the Germans took two men from every corner house on every street, shot them, and left their bodies in the front yard. We lived on a corner and so they shot my grandfather and one of my

Si Frumkin
3755 Goodland Avenue, Studio City, California 91604
(818) 984-1424
FAX (818) 766-4321

uncles.

When the ghetto was formed, there were close to 40,000 Jews in it. Three years later, when they transported us to Germany there were only 11,000 left.

The camp they took us to was for men only; the women were taken to another camp, in Poland. Our camp was a subdivision of Dachau - one of 10 camps with about 3000 prisoners in each, surrounding a gigantic construction project - an underground airplane factory. We worked 12 hour shifts, around the clock, never a day off, on a starvation diet. Every few weeks another transport would bring in a few hundred men to replace those who had died from exhaustion, hunger, or who had just given up.

I survived. I don't think that it was because I was smarter or braver than those who didn't. It was luck or fate, or a decision made for no rational reason, like the time when I decided to stay in the camp with my father, rather than be transported elsewhere with the other kids. A few weeks after we came to Dachau the Germans realized that there were about 60 boys among us who were under 16 - too young to live. We were told that all of us would be transferred to another camp to learn a skill like carpentry or metalworking, and then be assigned to factories or workshops. I hid when the trucks came to take the others away. 56 were taken that day, transported to Auschwitz to have medical experiments performed on them. There were no survivors.

My closest brush with death came when I was caught by an officer as I was emptying a bag of cement on the ground. We would cut a hole in the bottom of the paper bag, two more holes on the sides and wear the bag, under the striped prison jacket, like a sleeveless sweater, to keep out the winter cold. "Sabotage!", yelled the German as he grabbed me and pulled out his gun. I stood there, petrified, knowing only that I was about to die. Then someone called his name and he turned. "My God", he said to the other officer. "Fritz, I didn't know you were stationed here... It's good to see you again..." and as they shook hands and hugged, I turned and ran. They didn't follow.

Three others weren't as lucky. They too were accused of sabotage. They took a blanket that had belonged to a man who died, cut it into strips and wrapped them around their feet - it was winter and their boots had fallen apart. They were hanged, publicly, with all of us lined up at attention, watching.

But enough of this. These horror stories have been told time and time again and there is something else that I want to focus on, something that is seldom mentioned, a tragedy of neglect and indifference that eventually, decades later and continents away, prompted me to become involved in a cause that brought freedom to hundreds of thousands of persecuted human beings.

There were few suicides in the Nazi camps. There were those among us who had lost their will to live and lacked the strength to end it all - match stick limbs, shuffling along, never lifting their heads - and we knew that one day they wouldn't wake up or would just fall down and die quietly, eyes open and staring.

The rest of us lived one day at a time - another day, and then another one, and then, if we lasted, there would be liberation and a new beginning. No one thought beyond liberation - we were convinced that the world cared about

Si Frumkin
3755 Goodland Avenue, Studio City, California 91604
(818) 984-1424
FAX (818) 766-4321

us, that it would be happy that we survived, that there would be cheers and congratulations, and so we lived on, a day at a time.

I was 14 years old when I was liberated by the U.S. Army. My father died 2 weeks before.

The suicides began a month or two after liberation, after we were taken out of the camp and relocated in a deserted German army camp nearby. There was food, medical attention, clothing. No one beat or brutalized us, and although there were American sentries at the gate, we were free to go anywhere we liked. The problem was that there was no place to go.

The world was less than happy with us, the pitiful hundreds of thousands of Displaced Persons who had managed to survive. There was no country that welcomed us, no place we could go to escape the cursed German soil. In the Soviet Union all came before a commission that asked, "If Hitler decided to kill all Jews, why did they let you live? You must have collaborated with the nazis or you too would be dead, right? Well, if you are a friend of the nazis you are no friend of ours and, so, off to the gulag with you..."

United States was a closed country; it took in a few thousand but for most, the wait for the rest was 10, even 15 years. South America sold visas - if you had a few hundred dollars you could go there, but no one had any money. Australia, Canada, New Zealand, South Africa were unwilling to accept Jewish immigrants. The only place in the entire world that was willing to take in as many as wanted to come was Palestine - a British colony with a poor Jewish community of less than 600,000, but this too was closed by the British; the Royal Navy patrolled the Mediterranean, stopped the refugee boats that tried to sneak through, and imprisoned the passengers in a camp on Cyprus.

And so we realized that the world wasn't happy that we had survived. The world didn't know what to do with us. We were an embarrassment, a problem, a bother, and it would have been so much more satisfactory if we hadn't lived.

This was when the suicides began.

I wandered around Europe for a few years trying to catch up with the years of school I had missed. In 1949 I managed to be admitted to New York University and came to the States. In 1953 I graduated, got married and moved to California. On the surface, my life was almost humdrum - a house in the suburbs, a successful business, children...

For years, deep inside of me, I carried an anger against an indifferent world, the Allies who refused to bomb the death camps, the frontiers that were closed to Jews before, during, and after the Holocaust. And then, one day, I came to understand something both very profound and very simple - the world didn't hate me or my people or the survivors in general. The world didn't care about us simply because that is the way it is - the world just doesn't care *period*. Within the last decade millions of innocents were killed - Cambodia, Tibet, Afghanistan, Nigeria, Sudan, Ethiopia, Liberia, and elsewhere. Few cared. We worried about traffic jams, baseball scores, homework, and other trivia. Human lives meant as little in the 60s, 70s, and 80s as they did in the 30s and 40s. It wasn't fair, it wasn't right, it was disgusting, but that was the way it was...

Si Frumkin
3755 Goodland Avenue, Studio City, California 91604
(818) 984-1424
FAX (818) 766-4321

In 1969 I heard the message that changed my life. The message came from the Soviet Jews who constituted the 2nd largest Jewish community in the world and who were saying to anyone who would listen: "Why have you forgotten us?"

It was a powerful message and it touched a chord. I remembered the Displaced Persons camps in Germany when the world had forgotten about us, and I knew that something had to be done for the 3 million Soviet Jews - discriminated against, not allowed to study their history, their culture, speak their language, not allowed to live as Jews nor to leave the country where antisemitism was official policy.

In 1969 few people, myself included, knew about the problems of Soviet Jews. I had to learn from scratch and as I learned I realized that there were others like myself - caring, obsessed, willing to take on the Soviet superpower and force it to do what had been out of the question for the entire 50 years of its existence - permitting Soviet citizens to emigrate. I learned how to contact politicians, lead demonstrations, teach courses, make speeches, develop and print photographs, write press releases, use loudspeakers, be arrested, paint signs, walk picket lines, send books and other materials to Russia, and most of all, how to enlist people in this cause, how to project an image of power and massive popular support.

It took a long time, but the unthinkable happened. About 600,000 Soviet Jews have been allowed to exit to freedom over the last 20 years - as few as 500 in some years, as many as 200,000 last year. When the two superpowers met, the agenda more often than not included the Soviet Jewry question - in contrast to Allied indifference during the Holocaust. The world is aware of Soviet Jews - they may not know the details but just about everyone - Jew or gentile - knows that there is some kind of a problem there.

Most importantly, the message from the Soviet Union is no longer, "Why have you forgotten us?" They know that they haven't been forgotten after all.

And so, my friend, this is the story of both my deepest misfortune and my greatest triumph. I firmly believe that the most harmful phrase in any language is, "This is terrible! Someone should do something about it". Here's a news flash: there is no *someone*, he left last October and he is never coming back! There is only you and you can do whatever needs to be done, so don't wait for the *someone* - do it!

Sincerely,

Si Frumkin

"Nothing will ever be
attempted if all possible
objections must first be
overcome."

– Johnson

ROLF BENIRSCHKE

FORMER NFL PLACEKICKER
...set sixteen team records for the San Diego Chargers. He retired the third most accurate kicker in the history of the National Football League.

In the years since his NFL playing days Rolf Benirschke has become a sought-after motivational speaker, is the owner of Travel and Limousine Services in San Diego, and is a licensed insurance agent and partner in The Perkins Companies, a financial planning and insurance services company. In 1988, he was named host of NBC's popular daytime game show, "Wheel of Fortune." He co-starred with Vanna White until the show was sold to CBS in June, 1989.

In his letter, the illness Rolf writes of overcoming has been the focus of many magazine articles and television features. Because of the courageous way he dealt with that difficulty in his life, Rolf has since received numerous honors. Those include the NFL Man of the Year, the Comeback Player of the Year, the Philadelphia Sports Writers Association's "Most Courageous Athlete," and the NFL Players Association "Hero of the Year."

Among the causes he supports is the San Diego Zoo with his "Kicks for Critters" program, which he developed to help save endangered animals. The program has raised in excess of 1.3 million dollars.

Rolf was recently married to Mary Michaletz, a speech pathologist with a practice devoted mostly to helping youngsters with speech and language disabilities. They continue to live and work in San Diego.

GREAT COMEBACKS®

Rolf Benirschke
P.O. Box 9922
Rancho Santa Fee, CA 92067

Andy Andrews
P.O. Box 2761
Gulf Shores, AL 36547

Dear Andy,

I apologize for the delay in writing but, as you can imagine, things have been very busy lately. I am recently married and trying to move into a new house with my wife. It is all very exciting but does, somehow, make me wonder where all the time goes.

I appreciate your asking me to contribute a letter to your book, and share my struggle with inflammatory bowel disease (IBD). As you may remember, I became ill with ulcerative colitis early in my career as the placekicker for the San Diego Chargers. My symptoms came on very abruptly in the early part of the season in 1978 and worsened until, after four games in 1979, I collapsed on a flight home from a game. I required two surgeries within a week, and found myself weighing 123 pounds and wondering if I would live to walk out of the hospital.

The surgery had left me with an ileostomy, an opening in my abdomen where my waste drained into a bag. No professional football player had ever returned to the field after such a surgery, and few people seemed willing to talk about it. I found out, however, that there were close to 2 million people in America that were struggling with inflammatory bowel disease, either Crohn's disease or ulcerative colitis, and that the Crohn's and Colitis Foundation of America (formerly the National Foundation for Ileitis & Colitis, Inc.) was supporting these people and raising funds to find the cause and cure of the diseases.

Fortunately, I was put in contact with them and then visited by a young man from the United Ostomy Association (UOA). I quickly realized that having an ostomy shouldn't keep me from doing the things that I liked, and I began to wonder if I could play athletics again. At that point, the thought of playing football was still one I didn't dare consider. I had received hundreds of letters from people supporting me and wishing me well, and slowly I began to recognize that I had an opportunity to serve as an example for others if I could return to the field.

With the help of our strength coach and the support of my family and several teammates, I set about the long road to recovery. Initially, I couldn't do a sit-up, couldn't run 50 yards, and needed to gain back 50 pounds. Nonetheless, with my mother's advice, "that it takes one step at a time to climb the mountain," I began my comeback.

By the time training camp rolled around in 1980, I was ready to compete for my job, and see if I could kick again in the NFL. Fortunately, I played for Gene Klein and Don Coryell, an owner and coach who were willing to give me an opportunity when most other teams probably wouldn't. I was able to kick for seven more seasons and ended up playing in a Pro Bowl, being named Comeback Player of the Year and the NFL Man of the Year. It is humbling to think of what one can accomplish when one has faith in God, support of family and friends, and the desire to achieve something important.

Shortly after I returned to my placekicking job with the Chargers, I approached ConvaTec, a division of Bristol-Myers Squibb with the idea of forming a program to assist patients struggling with inflammatory bowel disease and/or ostomy surgery. The GREAT COMEBACKS® Award Program was created and continues to offer support to people across the country, and now around the world. We select annually a person who exemplifies what it takes to overcome these illnesses and hold that person up as a role model for others. We feel very fortunate to have the opportunity to reach others with our message, and look forward to the day when we have found the cause and cure for these diseases.

If you receive letters or telephone calls from people who have read this and would like to learn more about Crohn's disease or ulcerative colitis, or about our GREAT COMEBACKS® Award Program, please encourage them to write me at the above address. I have learned that although life doesn't always seem fair, it is always worth fighting for! Good luck with your book, Andy, and stay well.

With warm regards,

Rolf Benirschke

Rolf Benirschke

"All things are possible to
him who believes."

– *Mark 9:23*

CHARLIE FRYE

CLOWN / NEW VAUDEVILLIAN

...was a clown for Ringling Brothers/ Barnum and Bailey Circus. He and his wife, Sherry, now tour the United States, Europe, and the Orient as Charlie Frye and Company, one of the most popular specialty acts in the world.

Charlie Frye is one of those rare performers who, with a pure display of talent, literally elicits gasps from an audience. Juggling, sleight of hand, and a comic sense of the absurd are all displayed simultaneously. This blend of skill and slapstick, combined with a brilliant use of music has made Charlie Frye and Company well known the world over.

When I first saw Charlie and Sherry perform, it was on a cruise ship somewhere in the Caribbean. To say that I was impressed is an understatement of classic proportions. We have since become good friends, and I have become an even greater admirer of the people than of their talents. They also manage to graciously endure my pestering for private shows - they recently did one at my request in a dressing room for Kenny Rogers' crew!

Charlie has been compared to the likes of Stan Laurel, Charlie Chaplin, and Dick Van Dyke. On stage, he plays the part of the silent clown who adores his snooty wife/assistant, while performing feats of balance and accuracy that keep the audience laughing and applauding all at once.

Today, in addition to the occasional dressing room shows, Charlie Frye and Company dazzle audiences in Monte Carlo, Las Vegas, London, Paris, Atlantic City, South America, Canada, and Japan.

Dear Andy,

Thank you so much for offering to make my most discouraging and humiliating experiences public. Hey, what are friends for?

For me, being a clown with Ringling Bros. and Barnum & Bailey Circus was all I'd ever wanted. I had grown up performing in parades alongside my father and grandfather and had adopted their desire to take people's minds off their troubles. It's also a tremendous thrill to make people happy, as I'm sure you know.

The circus provided me with valuable training, wonderful friends, and my wife, Sherry. But after 3 years on the road I realized that this wasn't something I could afford to do the rest of my life. Especially when one of the veteran clowns strongly suggested that I go out on my own to try and make better use of my talents.

After my contract ran out, I ran away from the Circus and joined the "real world"---from the Greatest Show on Earth to parties on Long Island and juggling on the street with my hat out. What followed was the rejection and closed doors that New York is famous for. But, like they say, "God closes one door and opens another."

The door that opened was what we assumed to be our big break. A Las Vegas agent signed us for forty weeks of work a year. So we headed West, only to discover six months later that his promises were as empty as our bank account. When we heard his sales pitch---"These kids are desperate for work"--- we decided it was time to take our career in our own hands.

Finally we landed a job in a new show on the Strip. Two weeks later the entertainment director called to tell me the show was too long. He also told me he had solved the problem...we were fired. At least he gave us two weeks severance pay. Too bad the Casino cancelled the check.

I have always firmly believed that things work out for the best, but at this time my philosophy sounded naive. By now Sherry was ready to put on a Jeannie wig and wait tables at Caesars.

Two positive things did come out of the experience: the encouragement, friendship and criticism of George Carl---one of the world's greatest clowns; and a phone call from an agent in New York (where else?) who was looking for a comedy act to book on a cruise ship. I quickly informed him that he was in luck...we just happened to have an opening in our hectic schedule. Our ship had come in.

Charlie Frye   Las Vegas, Nevada   (702) 451-0365

Word of mouth began to spread and eventually we found ourselves in Atlantic City, Lake Tahoe, Monte Carlo and many other showrooms all over the world. And, yes, even in Las Vegas.

Sherry and I are currently working in France and then on to Switzerland. We've turned into modern day vaudevillians and are very happy, with our only regret being that we're too busy to get to see our friends, like you and Polly, more often. Things have indeed seemed to work out for the best, and in retrospect I've even come to appreciate most of my set-backs.

I recall one New York audition in particular. I desperately wanted the job and had I gotten it I'd probably still be wearing a chicken suit and performing at halftimes in New Jersey.

Love and laughter,

Charlie Frye

Charlie Frye   Las Vegas, Nevada   (702) 451-0365

"Thank God every
morning when you get
up that you have
something to do that day
which must be done,
whether you like it or
not. Being forced to work
and forced to do your
best will breed in you
temperance and self-
control; diligence and
strength of will;
cheerfulness and content;
and a hundred other
virtues the idle never
know."

– Kingsley

DICK
SCHAAP

AUTHOR/
SPORTSCASTER

...is an Emmy award winner and correspondent for "ABC's World News Tonight" and "20/20." He has authored twenty-six books including the best-selling sports book of all time, INSTANT REPLAY.

Dick Schaap is a specialist in the business of communication and his background is so broad and so successful, it is almost certainly unique. He has been city editor of a major metropolitan newspaper (NEW YORK HERALD TRIBUNE), senior editor of a major national magazine (NEWSWEEK), editor-in-chief of a national sports magazine (SPORT), author of twenty-six books, and correspondent for four major network television programs.

His study of the comedian Sid Caesar, a fifteen-minute profile which appeared on ABC's "20/20," won an Emmy in 1983. In addition, four of his sports reports which appeared on "World News Tonight," won Emmys in 1986.

Dick Schaap seems impervious to the blows of rejection. To a great degree, his letter reveals that attitude. And in his profession, like many others, that approach to problems can be a springboard to success.

Born in Brooklyn in 1934, Mr. Schaap graduated from Cornell University in 1955, then attended the Columbia University Graduate School of Journalism on a Grantland Rice Memorial Fellowship. He currently lives with his wife, Trish, and their children Kari and David, in the heart of New York City.

ABC NEWS
47 West 66th Street   New York, New York 10023-6290   (212) 887-7777

Mr. Andy Andrews
P.O. Box 2761
Gulf Shores, Alabama   36547

Dear Andy:

I have auditioned for a broadcasting job and not gotten it, I have been nominated
for an Emmy and not won it, I have suggested ideas for books, articles, and
television shows that have not been accepted, and yet, except perhaps for a few
teenaged romances, I don't feel that I have ever been personally rejected.

I reject my own ideas, my own work, all the time. I know better than anyone else
when my thoughts or my writings are not up to what I think is my standard. So
when other people reject my ideas or my work, I react by thinking one of four
things: They're right; they may be right; they may be wrong; or they're definitely
wrong. I can deal with all four of those rejections. I have the same range of
reactions to acceptance, to praise.

I guess I feel that without rejection and criticism, there is no acceptance, no
praise, nothing to measure the positive against.

I have written 28 books and 27 of them have been published. The one exception
was a biography of Teddy Kennedy, which I turned in just as his 1980 Presidential
campaign was falling apart. If the campaign had been flourishing, the publisher
would have accepted the manuscript. As it was, he saw no reason to publish the
book. Nor did I--except for my ego and my efforts, both of which were considerable.
I didn't take it personally.

Frank Sinatra, Joe DiMaggio and the late John L. Lewis have all rejected me--my
plea, anyway, for each of them to cooperate with me on an autobiography. (Joe
Namath, Bo Jackson and Billy Crystal, among others, have accepted me, have
worked with me on their autobiographies.) Again, I don't take it personally.
Sinatra, DiMaggio and Lewis rejected everyone who broached the subject of an
autobiography with them.

I don't think this is exactly the sort of experience you're looking for, so if
you reject this letter, I won't take it personally.

Best wishes.

Sincerely,

Dick Schaap

WILLIAM S. SESSIONS

DIRECTOR OF THE FBI

...previously a United States District Judge. He was sworn in as Director of the Federal Bureau of Investigation on November 2, 1987.

At a recent benefit performance in Washington, D.C., my wife, Polly, and I were fortunate enough to meet Director and Mrs. Sessions. One has only to spend a short time with the Director to be suitably impressed. He is a distinguished looking man who carries himself confidently. Warm and friendly, he and his wife Alice were among those hosting a dinner after the performance.

William S. Sessions was a private practitioner of law in Waco, Texas, from 1958 until 1969, when he left his firm to join the Department of Justice in Washington, D.C. as Chief of the Government Operations Section, Criminal Division. In 1971, he was appointed United States Attorney for the Western District of Texas.

In 1974, Director Sessions was appointed United States District Judge for the Western District of Texas, and in 1980, became Chief Judge of that court. He served on the Board of the Federal Judicial Center in Washington, D.C. and in committees of the State Bar of Texas and the Judicial Conference of the United States.

Always willing to "get the job done," his dedication and experience have propelled him to extraordinary success with the United States Department of Justice. The ability to lead and his determination to serve the public have made William S. Sessions the perfect man for the position of Director...of the FBI.

U.S. Department of Justice
Federal Bureau of Investigation

Office of the Director   *Washington, D.C. 20535*

Mr. and Mrs. Andy Andrews
Post Office Box 2761
Gulf Shores, Alabama   36547

Dear Andy and Polly,

Thank you for your letter of March 13th inviting me to send a "rejection" letter that might encourage others.

The one event that had more impact on my life than any other rejection, obstacle or failure came in the summer of 1946 when, as a 16-year-old, I contracted polio. From the outset, my disability was rather minor, that is, my upper right side including my shoulder, arm, and right hand became useless, but none of the doctors to whom I was taken in my hometown were able to diagnose the cause so I was finally taken to the world famous Mayo Clinic in Rochester, Minnesota, where the doctors diagnosed the polio. An appointment was immediately made for me at the Rehabilitation Center at St. Marys Hospital there in Rochester where I was to begin my treatment.

When I arrived the next morning, I walked, under my own power, through the doors leading to the Rehabilitation Center. What confronted me when I entered was absolutely stunning and stopped me in my tracks. What I saw was a dozen iron lung machines filled with young people for whom the machines were "breathing." Other young people with deformed and partially paralyzed bodies were struggling on parallel bars, padded stairways and other mechanical contraptions to help them regain the use of their body through massage, heat therapy and seemingly impossible exercises.

I watched this incredible scenario unfolding before me for a minute, burst into tears and left the room. Suddenly all of the bitterness and anger that had been welled up in me for the months since I had been afflicted were washed away, now I know, permanently, and was replaced by a deep and abiding gratitude for what God had spared me and a deep and abiding shame that I had so little appreciation of how truly fortunate I was.

That gratitude remains with me to this day so that not a day goes by but what I am reminded of how fortunate I am and that all of us have a continuing responsibility to be sensitive to and mindful of the needs of others.

Thank you for allowing me to share this experience with you and Polly.

Sincerely,

William S. Sessions
Director

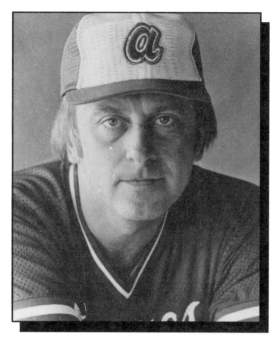

PHIL NIEKRO

FORMER MAJOR LEAGUE PITCHER

...is known to millions of baseball fans as "Knucksie." He is only the eighteenth pitcher in the history of Major League Baseball to reach the 300th-victory plateau.

Phil Niekro started his career as a free agent signee with the Milwaukee Braves organization in 1958. He spent nineteen years with the Braves, eighteen of those as an Atlanta Brave. He credits his father for putting the spark in his pitching by teaching him the knuckleball during a childhood game of catch. Bob Ueker, the former catcher turned broadcaster, also became invaluable. He was the first catcher to consistently get his mitt on Phil's unpredictable knuckler!

A great humanitarian, Phil Niekro raises funds for Spina Bifida, the second most common birth defect. He has aided March of Dimes, Big Brothers of America, and the Empty Stocking Fund.

Phil set several major league records, played in five All-Star games, and astonishingly, for a pitcher, won five Gold Glove Awards. He and his wife, Nancy, still live in Atlanta where Phil continues as an integral part of the Braves organization. Younger players, often in awe of him, are attempting what Phil Niekro has already accomplished. And not only do they now play in the shadow of the man - they play in the shadow of his statue, dedicated at the Atlanta Fulton County Stadium on October 2, 1986.

ATLANTA BRAVES
P. O. BOX 4064
ATLANTA, GA 30302

Mr. Andy Andrews
Post Office Box 2761
Gulf Shores, Alabama 36547

Dear Andy,

    Many people believe that the toughest times we face in our lives come while we are struggling for success. But I'm here to tell you that this isn't always the case. The toughest time in my life came as I was about to achieve the pinnacle of success. Several years ago, as the nation watched me prepare for my three-hundredth win, my heart was breaking. My father, you see, was on his deathbed several hundred miles away.

    With three days before my next start, Mom called my brother, Joe, and me back to Ohio. As she broke into tears, the nurse got on the phone and told us to hurry, that our dad was fading fast. Naturally, after talking to Billy Martin, our manager, and the Yankee owner, George Steinbrenner, we were on the next flight home.

    Dad held on for the next three days, forcing a decision I didn't want to make. Should I stay with my dad like I wanted to? Or should I go back to New York to try for the three-hundredth win. After leaning close to my father, and asking his advice, he asked for a piece of paper. Slowly and carefully he wrote on it: WIN / HAPPY. He was telling me to just win the game and he'd be happy.

    I flew back to New York with that piece of paper in my pocket. Landing only one hour and a half from game time, I rushed to the stadium, put on my uniform, and with Dad's paper still with me, went to warm up. After almost every pitch, I would look at it. "Win" it told me. Unfortunately, I did not win that game. Toronto beat us 5-2 and I was sure that my dad wouldn't make it until my next shot at three hundred.

    But he did. And I lost again. My father held on as I lost my next four starts. It seemed as if Dad were waiting for the milestone to be reached. And it seemed as if I'd never reach it!

All too soon, the last game of the season was at hand. I was scheduled to pitch. George Steinbrenner had a telephone hooked up in the hospital in Ohio to enable Dad and Mom to listen as I finally won my three-hundredth game...we won the game 9-0, making me, at age forty-eight, the oldest player in history to pitch a shutout.

Unbelievably, almost as soon as the game was over, Dad was released from Intensive Care. Later, as I gave the game ball to him and watched as he put it under his covers, I wondered if it wasn't only the winning that made him happy. Maybe it had more to do with plowing through the tough times, working when I didn't feel like working, and just getting the job done--no matter what it took.

I truly appreciate my father and the mental toughness, drive, and attitude he instilled in my brother and me. As a coal miner, he worked hard. He was proud of us and expected the best from us. And because of him, we expected the best from ourselves. Joe and I became the winningest brother combination in the history of major league baseball with 539 wins.

Sincerely,

Phil Niekro

"Great minds have
purposes, others have
wishes. Little minds are
tamed and subdued by
misfortunes; but great
minds rise above them."

– Washington Irving

ORVILLE REDENBACHER

ENTREPRENEUR

...now resides in San Diego with his wife, Nina. He manages to juggle a busy schedule of television commercials, interviews, and personal appearances on behalf of his Gourmet Popping Corn.

Our love affair with popcorn goes back centuries to the time when American Indians introduced it to the European colonists. But, just twenty-five years ago, one man's efforts helped change the "face of the kernel" for centuries to come! In 1965, Orville Redenbacher produced a hybrid variety of popping corn that popped up lighter, fluffier, and more consistently than any other. Yet, it didn't come without a lot of hard work and determination.

That hard work and determination is the subject of Mr. Redenbacher's letter. The time he spent and the knowledge he acquired along the way, quite literally changed the snacking habits of the nation!

The Orville Redenbacher's brand name now includes "Original Gourmet Popping Corn," "Gourmet Hot Air Popping Corn," "Gourmet White Popping Corn," "Gourmet Popping and Topping Buttery Flavor Oil," "Frozen Gourmet Microwave Popping Corn," "Gourmet Light Microwave Popping Corn" in two flavors, and "Gourmet Microwave Popping Corn" in eight different flavors.

Orville Redenbacher is still achieving the goals he sets for himself. He travels to promote his product, and at a point in his career where some would consider slowing down, Mr. Redenbacher wouldn't think of it. He's just too important to the business. After all, his face is as familiar as his popcorn.

ORVILLE REDENBACHER
1780 Avenida del Mundo, Apt. 704
Coronado, CA 92118

Andy Andrews
P. O. Box 2761
Gulf Shores, AL   36547

Dear Andy,

I was born in Clay County, Indiana in 1907. Our family raised
produce which, twice a week, we Redenbacher children would drive
to Terre Haute and sell door to door. I was the only one of the
four kids to get beyond the eighth grade, continuing on to Purdue
and majoring in agronomy. While at Purdue, I paid for my tuition
by scrubbing hog houses, feeding cattle, and tending chickens.

I had developed an affinity for popcorn back on our family farm
where it was our favorite snack and at Purdue became involved in
the research of hybrid popcorn seed. Becoming a millionaire was
the farthest thing from my mind. I just wanted to come up with
the best popcorn in the world!

After more than forty years of cross-breeding over 3,000 hybrids,
perseverance finally paid off. I came up with Orville Redenbacher's
Gourmet Popping Corn. It is fluffier and lighter than other
popping corns, and it has superior poppability -- at the end you're
left with virtually no unpopped kernels. Do you want to know the
secret? It is the exact moisture in each kernel -- 13.5%.

In 1976 I sold my Gourmet Popping Corn to Hunt-Wesson, Inc. and
it took only one year to become the number one selling popcorn
the United States -- a position it still holds today!

I suppose that persistence and stubbornness were responsible for
my success. For years and years I was told I was looking for a
will-o'-the-wisp, to leave well enough alone. I didn't listen.
When someone tells me something can't be done, that's exactly
what I'm going to do!

So follow the classic homespun principles. Never say die.
Never be satisfied. Be stubborn. Be persistent. Integrity
is a must. Anything worth having is worth striving for
with all your might. Does it sound corny? Honestly, Andy,
that's all there was to it for me. There were no magic
formulas!

                    Sincerely yours,

                    Orville Redenbacher
                    Orville Redenbacher

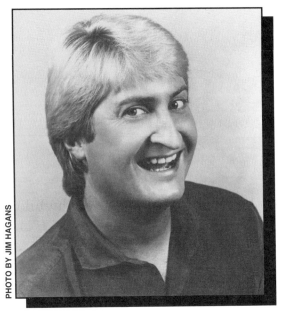

ANDY ANDREWS

ENTERTAINER

....became the first comedian ever allowed to record a live album at Caesars. The National Association for Campus Activities has named him "Entertainer of the Year" and "Comedian of the Year" - an award voted on by over 1000 colleges and universities nationwide.

WORDS FROM THE PUBLISHER

Andy Andrews...a comedian who is clean...receiving standing ovations! Words to this effect were broadcast by none other than Paul Harvey on the ABC radio network. VARIETY, THE LAS VEGAS SUN, and USA TODAY all agree – Andy Andrews is an entertainer enjoyed by all ages.

Because of his wide appeal, Andy is successful as a performer in Las Vegas, on college campuses, at conventions, on cruise ships, and in concert halls across America. He writes humorous fiction for magazines, stories for children, and regularly appears on national television.

"The Famous Fifty Parental Sayings" – one of his most popular routines– recently prompted President George Bush to say, "I want to thank Andy Andrews for teaching me how to deal with my grandchildren!" He made the remark on national television after watching Andy's performance at Ford's theater in Washington, D.C.

Andy Andrews is an entertainer with a true love for people. His primary goal, he confides, is to affect attitudes in a positive way...and with his concerts, recordings, and writing – he is doing just that!

Andy Andrews

| P.O. Box 2761 | ★ | Gulf Shores, Alabama 36547 |

Dear Friend,

As I am certain you already know, if something is worthwhile, it will rarely be easy. If it were easy--everyone would be doing it! I know this to be a true statement. In fact, I've known it for years. Why then, was I surprised when the very book that you are holding in your hands became the hardest thing I've ever done in my life?

It seems a simple enough concept, doesn't it? Ask someone to write a letter; then put the letter in a book. That was what I was thinking, too. It was a worthy project, I didn't foresee any problems getting people to participate. WRONG!

I WAS TURNED DOWN FIFTY-SIX TIMES BEFORE I RECEIVED THE FIRST LETTER!!!

Why, I wondered, was I being taught a lesson about rejection while I was trying to write a book about that very subject?! As more and more people said no, I began to have doubts. And as ashamed as I am to admit it now, I almost gave up. It just didn't seem realistic anymore. I had been working for almost nine months...and had one letter.

With encouragement from my wife, Polly, and my manager Robert Smith, I worked on. I decided to do what I could do, send out my requests, and leave the results to God. He knew who was to be in this book, I reasoned...it was my job to find them!

Soon, I had changed my thinking. I was calm when someone told me "no." It only made my working list shorter! I actually became proud of some of my rejections--a few of which were hilarious. An athlete wrote me a full page letter explaining why he didn't have time to write me a letter (Mark Spitz). A newspaper columnist sent back my letter of request and on it, in longhand, she had written, "I have never been rejected!" (Abigail Van Buren). And then there was the attorney whose letter commanded that I not even mention his client's name (Joe DiMaggio. Joe DiMaggio. Joe DiMaggio).

Meanwhile, the "good" letters trickled in. Only three times did I receive two in one day. But as they arrived, I became more and more convinced that the words so carefully written by these people had to be shared with you. I often got chills as I read about the problems of someone I had admired for years. And I was often embarrassed as I reflected on things I had at one time considered "major" problems in my own life.

Now, after almost two years of contacting over six hundred people, the book is complete. I have seen once again that if something is worthwhile, it will rarely be easy! The lessons I have learned from the people who shared their STORMS OF PERFECTION will continue to inspire and encourage me. And it is my hope for you, that as you read these letters again and again, your own life will seize the courage and hope they contain. Remember: the only limit to what you can accomplish is the width of your ideas and the depth of your dedication!

Sincerely yours,

Andy Andrews

Andy Andrews

AA: bp

The following companion products are also available
from Lightning Crown Publishing.

Book – <u>Storms Of Perfection</u> $12.95

Cassette: "Storms Of Perfection –   9.95
Words Of Inspiration" *A 40-minute*
live presentation by Andy Andrews
A companion to the book <u>*Storms of Perfection*</u>

Cassette: "Andy Andrews 'Live'   9.95
Caesars Tahoe"
35 minutes of comedy in Andy's own unique style

Video: "Off The Road With Andy Andrews"   24.95
A Lighthearted Tour Of Nashville
Great for children of all ages – 60 min. VHS only

Aqua Nite Shirt: Fifty Famous
Parental Sayings *(One Size Fits All)*   16.95
Andy's best known routine printed in bright
colors on a roomy nite shirt

White T-Shirt: Fifty Famous
Parental Sayings *(L & XL)*   13.95
Andy's best known routine printed in bright colors

Write for more information to:
ANDY ANDREWS' MERCHANDISE
P.O. Box 17321
Nashville, TN 37217

INDEX